Marketing: A Very Short Introduction

Very Short Introductions available now:

ABOLITIONISM Richard S. Newman
THE ABRAHAMIC RELIGIONS
    Charles L. Cohen
ACCOUNTING Christopher Nobes
ADAM SMITH Christopher J. Berry
ADOLESCENCE Peter K. Smith
ADVERTISING Winston Fletcher
AERIAL WARFARE Frank Ledwidge
AESTHETICS Bence Nanay
AFRICAN AMERICAN
    RELIGION Eddie S. Glaude Jr
AFRICAN HISTORY John Parker and
    Richard Rathbone
AFRICAN POLITICS Ian Taylor
AFRICAN RELIGIONS
    Jacob K. Olupona
AGEING Nancy A. Pachana
AGNOSTICISM Robin Le Poidevin
AGRICULTURE Paul Brassley and
    Richard Soffe
ALBERT CAMUS Oliver Gloag
ALEXANDER THE GREAT
    Hugh Bowden
ALGEBRA Peter M. Higgins
AMERICAN BUSINESS HISTORY
    Walter A. Friedman
AMERICAN CULTURAL HISTORY
    Eric Avila
AMERICAN FOREIGN
    RELATIONS Andrew Preston
AMERICAN HISTORY Paul S. Boyer
AMERICAN IMMIGRATION
    David A. Gerber
AMERICAN LEGAL HISTORY
    G. Edward White

AMERICAN MILITARY HISTORY
    Joseph T. Glatthaar
AMERICAN NAVAL HISTORY
    Craig L. Symonds
AMERICAN POLITICAL HISTORY
    Donald Critchlow
AMERICAN POLITICAL PARTIES
    AND ELECTIONS L. Sandy Maisel
AMERICAN POLITICS
    Richard M. Valelly
THE AMERICAN PRESIDENCY
    Charles O. Jones
THE AMERICAN REVOLUTION
    Robert J. Allison
AMERICAN SLAVERY
    Heather Andrea Williams
THE AMERICAN WEST Stephen Aron
AMERICAN WOMEN'S
    HISTORY Susan Ware
ANAESTHESIA Aidan O'Donnell
ANALYTIC PHILOSOPHY
    Michael Beaney
ANARCHISM Colin Ward
ANCIENT ASSYRIA Karen Radner
ANCIENT EGYPT Ian Shaw
ANCIENT EGYPTIAN ART AND
    ARCHITECTURE Christina Riggs
ANCIENT GREECE Paul Cartledge
THE ANCIENT NEAR EAST
    Amanda H. Podany
ANCIENT PHILOSOPHY Julia Annas
ANCIENT WARFARE Harry Sidebottom
ANGELS David Albert Jones
ANGLICANISM Mark Chapman
THE ANGLO-SAXON AGE John Blair

ANIMAL BEHAVIOUR
Tristram D. Wyatt
THE ANIMAL KINGDOM
Peter Holland
ANIMAL RIGHTS David DeGrazia
THE ANTARCTIC Klaus Dodds
ANTHROPOCENE Erle C. Ellis
ANTISEMITISM Steven Beller
ANXIETY Daniel Freeman and
Jason Freeman
THE APOCRYPHAL GOSPELS
Paul Foster
APPLIED MATHEMATICS
Alain Goriely
ARCHAEOLOGY Paul Bahn
ARCHITECTURE Andrew Ballantyne
ARISTOCRACY William Doyle
ARISTOTLE Jonathan Barnes
ART HISTORY Dana Arnold
ART THEORY Cynthia Freeland
ARTIFICIAL INTELLIGENCE
Margaret A. Boden
ASIAN AMERICAN HISTORY
Madeline Y. Hsu
ASTROBIOLOGY David C. Catling
ASTROPHYSICS James Binney
ATHEISM Julian Baggini
THE ATMOSPHERE Paul I. Palmer
AUGUSTINE Henry Chadwick
AUSTRALIA Kenneth Morgan
AUTISM Uta Frith
AUTOBIOGRAPHY Laura Marcus
THE AVANT GARDE David Cottington
THE AZTECS David Carrasco
BABYLONIA Trevor Bryce
BACTERIA Sebastian G. B. Amyes
BANKING John Goddard and
John O. S. Wilson
BARTHES Jonathan Culler
THE BEATS David Sterritt
BEAUTY Roger Scruton
BEHAVIOURAL ECONOMICS
Michelle Baddeley
BESTSELLERS John Sutherland
THE BIBLE John Riches
BIBLICAL ARCHAEOLOGY
Eric H. Cline
BIG DATA Dawn E. Holmes
BIOGEOGRAPHY Mark V. Lomolino
BIOGRAPHY Hermione Lee
BIOMETRICS Michael Fairhurst

BLACK HOLES Katherine Blundell
BLOOD Chris Cooper
THE BLUES Elijah Wald
THE BODY Chris Shilling
THE BOOK OF COMMON
PRAYER Brian Cummings
THE BOOK OF MORMON
Terryl Givens
BORDERS Alexander C. Diener and
Joshua Hagen
THE BRAIN Michael O'Shea
BRANDING Robert Jones
THE BRICS Andrew F. Cooper
THE BRITISH CONSTITUTION
Martin Loughlin
THE BRITISH EMPIRE Ashley Jackson
BRITISH POLITICS Tony Wright
BUDDHA Michael Carrithers
BUDDHISM Damien Keown
BUDDHIST ETHICS Damien Keown
BYZANTIUM Peter Sarris
C. S. LEWIS James Como
CALVINISM Jon Balserak
CANADA Donald Wright
CANCER Nicholas James
CAPITALISM James Fulcher
CATHOLICISM Gerald O'Collins
CAUSATION Stephen Mumford and
Rani Lill Anjum
THE CELL Terence Allen and
Graham Cowling
THE CELTS Barry Cunliffe
CHAOS Leonard Smith
CHARLES DICKENS Jenny Hartley
CHEMISTRY Peter Atkins
CHILD PSYCHOLOGY Usha Goswami
CHILDREN'S LITERATURE
Kimberley Reynolds
CHINESE LITERATURE
Sabina Knight
CHOICE THEORY Michael Allingham
CHRISTIAN ART Beth Williamson
CHRISTIAN ETHICS D. Stephen Long
CHRISTIANITY Linda Woodhead
CIRCADIAN RHYTHMS
Russell Foster and Leon Kreitzman
CITIZENSHIP Richard Bellamy
CIVIL ENGINEERING David Muir Wood
CLASSICAL LITERATURE William Allan
CLASSICAL MYTHOLOGY
Helen Morales

CLASSICS Mary Beard and
  John Henderson
CLAUSEWITZ Michael Howard
CLIMATE Mark Maslin
CLIMATE CHANGE Mark Maslin
CLINICAL PSYCHOLOGY
  Susan Llewelyn and
  Katie Aafjes-van Doorn
COGNITIVE NEUROSCIENCE
  Richard Passingham
THE COLD WAR Robert McMahon
COLONIAL AMERICA Alan Taylor
COLONIAL LATIN AMERICAN
  LITERATURE Rolena Adorno
COMBINATORICS Robin Wilson
COMEDY Matthew Bevis
COMMUNISM Leslie Holmes
COMPARATIVE LITERATURE
  Ben Hutchinson
COMPLEXITY John H. Holland
THE COMPUTER Darrel Ince
COMPUTER SCIENCE
  Subrata Dasgupta
CONCENTRATION CAMPS
  Dan Stone
CONFUCIANISM Daniel K. Gardner
THE CONQUISTADORS
  Matthew Restall and
  Felipe Fernández-Armesto
CONSCIENCE Paul Strohm
CONSCIOUSNESS Susan Blackmore
CONTEMPORARY ART
  Julian Stallabrass
CONTEMPORARY FICTION
  Robert Eaglestone
CONTINENTAL PHILOSOPHY
  Simon Critchley
COPERNICUS Owen Gingerich
CORAL REEFS Charles Sheppard
CORPORATE SOCIAL
  RESPONSIBILITY Jeremy Moon
CORRUPTION Leslie Holmes
COSMOLOGY Peter Coles
COUNTRY MUSIC Richard Carlin
CRIME FICTION Richard Bradford
CRIMINAL JUSTICE Julian V. Roberts
CRIMINOLOGY Tim Newburn
CRITICAL THEORY
  Stephen Eric Bronner
THE CRUSADES Christopher Tyerman

CRYPTOGRAPHY Fred Piper and
  Sean Murphy
CRYSTALLOGRAPHY A. M. Glazer
THE CULTURAL REVOLUTION
  Richard Curt Kraus
DADA AND SURREALISM
  David Hopkins
DANTE Peter Hainsworth and
  David Robey
DARWIN Jonathan Howard
THE DEAD SEA SCROLLS
  Timothy H. Lim
DECADENCE David Weir
DECOLONIZATION Dane Kennedy
DEMENTIA Kathleen Taylor
DEMOCRACY Bernard Crick
DEMOGRAPHY Sarah Harper
DEPRESSION Jan Scott and
  Mary Jane Tacchi
DERRIDA Simon Glendinning
DESCARTES Tom Sorell
DESERTS Nick Middleton
DESIGN John Heskett
DEVELOPMENT Ian Goldin
DEVELOPMENTAL BIOLOGY
  Lewis Wolpert
THE DEVIL Darren Oldridge
DIASPORA Kevin Kenny
DICTIONARIES Lynda Mugglestone
DINOSAURS David Norman
DIPLOMACY Joseph M. Siracusa
DOCUMENTARY FILM
  Patricia Aufderheide
DREAMING J. Allan Hobson
DRUGS Les Iversen
DRUIDS Barry Cunliffe
DYNASTY Jeroen Duindam
DYSLEXIA Margaret J. Snowling
EARLY MUSIC Thomas Forrest Kelly
THE EARTH Martin Redfern
EARTH SYSTEM SCIENCE Tim Lenton
ECOLOGY Jaboury Ghazoul
ECONOMICS Partha Dasgupta
EDUCATION Gary Thomas
EGYPTIAN MYTH Geraldine Pinch
EIGHTEENTH-CENTURY
  BRITAIN Paul Langford
THE ELEMENTS Philip Ball
ÉMILE ZOLA Brian Nelson
EMOTION Dylan Evans

EMPIRE Stephen Howe
ENERGY SYSTEMS Nick Jenkins
ENGELS Terrell Carver
ENGINEERING David Blockley
THE ENGLISH LANGUAGE
    Simon Horobin
ENGLISH LITERATURE Jonathan Bate
THE ENLIGHTENMENT
    John Robertson
ENTREPRENEURSHIP
    Paul Westhead and Mike Wright
ENVIRONMENTAL
    ECONOMICS Stephen Smith
ENVIRONMENTAL ETHICS
    Robin Attfield
ENVIRONMENTAL LAW
    Elizabeth Fisher
ENVIRONMENTAL POLITICS
    Andrew Dobson
ENZYMES Paul Engel
EPICUREANISM Catherine Wilson
EPIDEMIOLOGY Rodolfo Saracci
ETHICS Simon Blackburn
ETHNOMUSICOLOGY Timothy Rice
THE ETRUSCANS Christopher Smith
EUGENICS Philippa Levine
THE EUROPEAN UNION
    Simon Usherwood and John Pinder
EUROPEAN UNION LAW
    Anthony Arnull
EVOLUTION Brian and
    Deborah Charlesworth
EXISTENTIALISM Thomas Flynn
EXPLORATION Stewart A. Weaver
EXTINCTION Paul B. Wignall
THE EYE Michael Land
FAIRY TALE Marina Warner
FAMILY LAW Jonathan Herring
FASCISM Kevin Passmore
FASHION Rebecca Arnold
FEDERALISM Mark J. Rozell and
    Clyde Wilcox
FEMINISM Margaret Walters
FILM Michael Wood
FILM MUSIC Kathryn Kalinak
FILM NOIR James Naremore
FIRE Andrew C. Scott
THE FIRST WORLD WAR
    Michael Howard
FOLK MUSIC Mark Slobin

FOOD John Krebs
FORENSIC PSYCHOLOGY
    David Canter
FORENSIC SCIENCE Jim Fraser
FORESTS Jaboury Ghazoul
FOSSILS Keith Thomson
FOUCAULT Gary Gutting
THE FOUNDING FATHERS
    R. B. Bernstein
FRACTALS Kenneth Falconer
FREE SPEECH Nigel Warburton
FREE WILL Thomas Pink
FREEMASONRY Andreas Önnerfors
FRENCH LITERATURE John D. Lyons
FRENCH PHILOSOPHY
    Stephen Gaukroger and Knox Peden
THE FRENCH REVOLUTION
    William Doyle
FREUD Anthony Storr
FUNDAMENTALISM Malise Ruthven
FUNGI Nicholas P. Money
THE FUTURE Jennifer M. Gidley
GALAXIES John Gribbin
GALILEO Stillman Drake
GAME THEORY Ken Binmore
GANDHI Bhikhu Parekh
GARDEN HISTORY Gordon Campbell
GENES Jonathan Slack
GENIUS Andrew Robinson
GENOMICS John Archibald
GEOFFREY CHAUCER David Wallace
GEOGRAPHY John Matthews and
    David Herbert
GEOLOGY Jan Zalasiewicz
GEOPHYSICS William Lowrie
GEOPOLITICS Klaus Dodds
GEORGE BERNARD
    SHAW Christopher Wixson
GERMAN LITERATURE Nicholas Boyle
GERMAN PHILOSOPHY
    Andrew Bowie
THE GHETTO Bryan Cheyette
GLACIATION David J. A. Evans
GLOBAL CATASTROPHES Bill McGuire
GLOBAL ECONOMIC HISTORY
    Robert C. Allen
GLOBAL ISLAM Nile Green
GLOBALIZATION Manfred B. Steger
GOD John Bowker
GOETHE Ritchie Robertson

THE GOTHIC Nick Groom
GOVERNANCE Mark Bevir
GRAVITY Timothy Clifton
THE GREAT DEPRESSION AND THE
    NEW DEAL Eric Rauchway
HABERMAS James Gordon Finlayson
THE HABSBURG EMPIRE
    Martyn Rady
HAPPINESS Daniel M. Haybron
THE HARLEM RENAISSANCE
    Cheryl A. Wall
THE HEBREW BIBLE AS
    LITERATURE Tod Linafelt
HEGEL Peter Singer
HEIDEGGER Michael Inwood
THE HELLENISTIC AGE
    Peter Thonemann
HEREDITY John Waller
HERMENEUTICS Jens Zimmermann
HERODOTUS Jennifer T. Roberts
HIEROGLYPHS Penelope Wilson
HINDUISM Kim Knott
HISTORY John H. Arnold
THE HISTORY OF ASTRONOMY
    Michael Hoskin
THE HISTORY OF CHEMISTRY
    William H. Brock
THE HISTORY OF CHILDHOOD
    James Marten
THE HISTORY OF CINEMA
    Geoffrey Nowell-Smith
THE HISTORY OF LIFE
    Michael Benton
THE HISTORY OF MATHEMATICS
    Jacqueline Stedall
THE HISTORY OF MEDICINE
    William Bynum
THE HISTORY OF PHYSICS
    J. L. Heilbron
THE HISTORY OF TIME
    Leofranc Holford-Strevens
HIV AND AIDS Alan Whiteside
HOBBES Richard Tuck
HOLLYWOOD Peter Decherney
THE HOLY ROMAN EMPIRE
    Joachim Whaley
HOME Michael Allen Fox
HOMER Barbara Graziosi
HORMONES Martin Luck
HUMAN ANATOMY Leslie Klenerman
HUMAN EVOLUTION Bernard Wood

HUMAN RIGHTS Andrew Clapham
HUMANISM Stephen Law
HUME A. J. Ayer
HUMOUR Noël Carroll
THE ICE AGE Jamie Woodward
IDENTITY Florian Coulmas
IDEOLOGY Michael Freeden
THE IMMUNE SYSTEM
    Paul Klenerman
INDIAN CINEMA Ashish Rajadhyaksha
INDIAN PHILOSOPHY Sue Hamilton
THE INDUSTRIAL REVOLUTION
    Robert C. Allen
INFECTIOUS DISEASE Marta L. Wayne
    and Benjamin M. Bolker
INFINITY Ian Stewart
INFORMATION Luciano Floridi
INNOVATION Mark Dodgson and
    David Gann
INTELLECTUAL PROPERTY
    Siva Vaidhyanathan
INTELLIGENCE Ian J. Deary
INTERNATIONAL LAW
    Vaughan Lowe
INTERNATIONAL MIGRATION
    Khalid Koser
INTERNATIONAL RELATIONS
    Christian Reus-Smit
INTERNATIONAL SECURITY
    Christopher S. Browning
IRAN Ali M. Ansari
ISLAM Malise Ruthven
ISLAMIC HISTORY Adam Silverstein
ILAMIC LAW Mashood A. Baderin
ISOTOPES Rob Ellam
ITALIAN LITERATURE
    Peter Hainsworth and David Robey
JESUS Richard Bauckham
JEWISH HISTORY David N. Myers
JOURNALISM Ian Hargreaves
JUDAISM Norman Solomon
JUNG Anthony Stevens
KABBALAH Joseph Dan
KAFKA Ritchie Robertson
KANT Roger Scruton
KEYNES Robert Skidelsky
KIERKEGAARD Patrick Gardiner
KNOWLEDGE Jennifer Nagel
THE KORAN Michael Cook
KOREA Michael J. Seth
LAKES Warwick F. Vincent

LANDSCAPE ARCHITECTURE
Ian H. Thompson
LANDSCAPES AND
GEOMORPHOLOGY
Andrew Goudie and Heather Viles
LANGUAGES Stephen R. Anderson
LATE ANTIQUITY Gillian Clark
LAW Raymond Wacks
THE LAWS OF THERMODYNAMICS
Peter Atkins
LEADERSHIP Keith Grint
LEARNING Mark Haselgrove
LEIBNIZ Maria Rosa Antognazza
LEO TOLSTOY Liza Knapp
LIBERALISM Michael Freeden
LIGHT Ian Walmsley
LINCOLN Allen C. Guelzo
LINGUISTICS Peter Matthews
LITERARY THEORY Jonathan Culler
LOCKE John Dunn
LOGIC Graham Priest
LOVE Ronald de Sousa
MACHIAVELLI Quentin Skinner
MADNESS Andrew Scull
MAGIC Owen Davies
MAGNA CARTA Nicholas Vincent
MAGNETISM Stephen Blundell
MALTHUS Donald Winch
MAMMALS T. S. Kemp
MANAGEMENT John Hendry
MAO Delia Davin
MARINE BIOLOGY Philip V. Mladenov
MARKETING
Kenneth Le Meunier-FitzHugh
THE MARQUIS DE SADE John Phillips
MARTIN LUTHER Scott H. Hendrix
MARTYRDOM Jolyon Mitchell
MARX Peter Singer
MATERIALS Christopher Hall
MATHEMATICAL FINANCE
Mark H. A. Davis
MATHEMATICS Timothy Gowers
MATTER Geoff Cottrell
THE MAYA Matthew Restall and
Amara Solari
THE MEANING OF LIFE
Terry Eagleton
MEASUREMENT David Hand
MEDICAL ETHICS Michael Dunn and
Tony Hope

MEDICAL LAW Charles Foster
MEDIEVAL BRITAIN John Gillingham
and Ralph A. Griffiths
MEDIEVAL LITERATURE
Elaine Treharne
MEDIEVAL PHILOSOPHY
John Marenbon
MEMORY Jonathan K. Foster
METAPHYSICS Stephen Mumford
METHODISM William J. Abraham
THE MEXICAN REVOLUTION
Alan Knight
MICHAEL FARADAY
Frank A. J. L. James
MICROBIOLOGY Nicholas P. Money
MICROECONOMICS Avinash Dixit
MICROSCOPY Terence Allen
THE MIDDLE AGES Miri Rubin
MILITARY JUSTICE Eugene R. Fidell
MILITARY STRATEGY
Antulio J. Echevarria II
MINERALS David Vaughan
MIRACLES Yujin Nagasawa
MODERN ARCHITECTURE
Adam Sharr
MODERN ART David Cottington
MODERN CHINA Rana Mitter
MODERN DRAMA
Kirsten E. Shepherd-Barr
MODERN FRANCE
Vanessa R. Schwartz
MODERN INDIA Craig Jeffrey
MODERN IRELAND Senia Pašeta
MODERN ITALY Anna Cento Bull
MODERN JAPAN
Christopher Goto-Jones
MODERN LATIN
AMERICAN LITERATURE
Roberto González Echevarría
MODERN WAR Richard English
MODERNISM Christopher Butler
MOLECULAR BIOLOGY Aysha Divan
and Janice A. Royds
MOLECULES Philip Ball
MONASTICISM Stephen J. Davis
THE MONGOLS Morris Rossabi
MONTAIGNE William M. Hamlin
MOONS David A. Rothery
MORMONISM
Richard Lyman Bushman

MOUNTAINS Martin F. Price
MUHAMMAD Jonathan A. C. Brown
MULTICULTURALISM Ali Rattansi
MULTILINGUALISM John C. Maher
MUSIC Nicholas Cook
MYTH Robert A. Segal
NAPOLEON David Bell
THE NAPOLEONIC WARS
    Mike Rapport
NATIONALISM Steven Grosby
NATIVE AMERICAN LITERATURE
    Sean Teuton
NAVIGATION Jim Bennett
NAZI GERMANY Jane Caplan
NELSON MANDELA Elleke Boehmer
NEOLIBERALISM Manfred B. Steger
    and Ravi K. Roy
NETWORKS Guido Caldarelli and
    Michele Catanzaro
THE NEW TESTAMENT Luke
    Timothy Johnson
THE NEW TESTAMENT AS
    LITERATURE Kyle Keefer
NEWTON Robert Iliffe
NIELS BOHR J. L. Heilbron
NIETZSCHE Michael Tanner
NINETEENTH-CENTURY BRITAIN
    Christopher Harvie and
    H. C. G. Matthew
THE NORMAN CONQUEST
    George Garnett
NORTH AMERICAN INDIANS
    Theda Perdue and Michael D. Green
NORTHERN IRELAND
    Marc Mulholland
NOTHING Frank Close
NUCLEAR PHYSICS Frank Close
NUCLEAR POWER Maxwell Irvine
NUCLEAR WEAPONS
    Joseph M. Siracusa
NUMBER THEORY Robin Wilson
NUMBERS Peter M. Higgins
NUTRITION David A. Bender
OBJECTIVITY Stephen Gaukroger
OCEANS Dorrik Stow
THE OLD TESTAMENT
    Michael D. Coogan
THE ORCHESTRA D. Kern Holoman
ORGANIC CHEMISTRY
    Graham Patrick
ORGANIZATIONS Mary Jo Hatch
ORGANIZED CRIME
    Georgios A. Antonopoulos and
    Georgios Papanicolaou
ORTHODOX CHRISTIANITY
    A. Edward Siecienski
OVID Llewelyn Morgan
PAGANISM Owen Davies
PAIN Rob Boddice
THE PALESTINIAN-ISRAELI
    CONFLICT Martin Bunton
PANDEMICS Christian W. McMillen
PARTICLE PHYSICS Frank Close
PAUL E. P. Sanders
PEACE Oliver P. Richmond
PENTECOSTALISM William K. Kay
PERCEPTION Brian Rogers
THE PERIODIC TABLE Eric R. Scerri
PHILOSOPHICAL METHOD
    Timothy Williamson
PHILOSOPHY Edward Craig
PHILOSOPHY IN THE ISLAMIC
    WORLD Peter Adamson
PHILOSOPHY OF BIOLOGY
    Samir Okasha
PHILOSOPHY OF LAW
    Raymond Wacks
PHILOSOPHY OF SCIENCE
    Samir Okasha
PHILOSOPHY OF RELIGION
    Tim Bayne
PHOTOGRAPHY Steve Edwards
PHYSICAL CHEMISTRY Peter Atkins
PHYSICS Sidney Perkowitz
PILGRIMAGE Ian Reader
PLAGUE Paul Slack
PLANETS David A. Rothery
PLANTS Timothy Walker
PLATE TECTONICS Peter Molnar
PLATO Julia Annas
POETRY Bernard O'Donoghue
POLITICAL PHILOSOPHY David Miller
POLITICS Kenneth Minogue
POPULISM Cas Mudde and
    Cristóbal Rovira Kaltwasser
POSTCOLONIALISM Robert Young
POSTMODERNISM Christopher Butler
POSTSTRUCTURALISM
    Catherine Belsey
POVERTY Philip N. Jefferson

PREHISTORY Chris Gosden
PRESOCRATIC PHILOSOPHY
    Catherine Osborne
PRIVACY Raymond Wacks
PROBABILITY John Haigh
PROGRESSIVISM Walter Nugent
PROHIBITION W. J. Rorabaugh
PROJECTS Andrew Davies
PROTESTANTISM Mark A. Noll
PSYCHIATRY Tom Burns
PSYCHOANALYSIS Daniel Pick
PSYCHOLOGY Gillian Butler and
    Freda McManus
PSYCHOLOGY OF MUSIC
    Elizabeth Hellmuth Margulis
PSYCHOPATHY Essi Viding
PSYCHOTHERAPY Tom Burns and
    Eva Burns-Lundgren
PUBLIC ADMINISTRATION
    Stella Z. Theodoulou and Ravi K. Roy
PUBLIC HEALTH Virginia Berridge
PURITANISM Francis J. Bremer
THE QUAKERS Pink Dandelion
QUANTUM THEORY
    John Polkinghorne
RACISM Ali Rattansi
RADIOACTIVITY Claudio Tuniz
RASTAFARI Ennis B. Edmonds
READING Belinda Jack
THE REAGAN REVOLUTION Gil Troy
REALITY Jan Westerhoff
RECONSTRUCTION Allen C. Guelzo
THE REFORMATION Peter Marshall
RELATIVITY Russell Stannard
RELIGION Thomas A. Tweed
RELIGION IN AMERICA
    Timothy Beal
THE RENAISSANCE Jerry Brotton
RENAISSANCE ART
    Geraldine A. Johnson
RENEWABLE ENERGY Nick Jelley
REPTILES T. S. Kemp
REVOLUTIONS Jack A. Goldstone
RHETORIC Richard Toye
RISK Baruch Fischhoff and John Kadvany
RITUAL Barry Stephenson
RIVERS Nick Middleton
ROBOTICS Alan Winfield
ROCKS Jan Zalasiewicz
ROMAN BRITAIN Peter Salway
THE ROMAN EMPIRE
    Christopher Kelly
THE ROMAN REPUBLIC
    David M. Gwynn
ROMANTICISM Michael Ferber
ROUSSEAU Robert Wokler
RUSSELL A. C. Grayling
THE RUSSIAN ECONOMY
    Richard Connolly
RUSSIAN HISTORY Geoffrey Hosking
RUSSIAN LITERATURE Catriona Kelly
THE RUSSIAN REVOLUTION
    S. A. Smith
SAINTS Simon Yarrow
SAVANNAS Peter A. Furley
SCEPTICISM Duncan Pritchard
SCHIZOPHRENIA Chris Frith and
    Eve Johnstone
SCHOPENHAUER
    Christopher Janaway
SCIENCE AND RELIGION
    Thomas Dixon
SCIENCE FICTION David Seed
THE SCIENTIFIC REVOLUTION
    Lawrence M. Principe
SCOTLAND Rab Houston
SECULARISM Andrew Copson
SEXUAL SELECTION Marlene Zuk and
    Leigh W. Simmons
SEXUALITY Véronique Mottier
SHAKESPEARE'S COMEDIES
    Bart van Es
SHAKESPEARE'S SONNETS AND
    POEMS Jonathan F. S. Post
SHAKESPEARE'S TRAGEDIES
    Stanley Wells
SIKHISM Eleanor Nesbitt
THE SILK ROAD James A. Millward
SLANG Jonathon Green
SLEEP Steven W. Lockley and
    Russell G. Foster
SMELL Matthew Cobb
SOCIAL AND CULTURAL
    ANTHROPOLOGY John Monaghan
    and Peter Just
SOCIAL PSYCHOLOGY Richard J. Crisp
SOCIAL WORK Sally Holland and
    Jonathan Scourfield
SOCIALISM Michael Newman
SOCIOLINGUISTICS John Edwards

SOCIOLOGY Steve Bruce
SOCRATES C. C. W. Taylor
SOFT MATTER Tom McLeish
SOUND Mike Goldsmith
SOUTHEAST ASIA James R. Rush
THE SOVIET UNION Stephen Lovell
THE SPANISH CIVIL WAR
    Helen Graham
SPANISH LITERATURE Jo Labanyi
SPINOZA Roger Scruton
SPIRITUALITY Philip Sheldrake
SPORT Mike Cronin
STARS Andrew King
STATISTICS David J. Hand
STEM CELLS Jonathan Slack
STOICISM Brad Inwood
STRUCTURAL ENGINEERING
    David Blockley
STUART BRITAIN John Morrill
THE SUN Philip Judge
SUPERCONDUCTIVITY
    Stephen Blundell
SUPERSTITION Stuart Vyse
SYMMETRY Ian Stewart
SYNAESTHESIA Julia Simner
SYNTHETIC BIOLOGY Jamie A. Davies
SYSTEMS BIOLOGY Eberhard O. Voit
TAXATION Stephen Smith
TEETH Peter S. Ungar
TELESCOPES Geoff Cottrell
TERRORISM Charles Townshend
THEATRE Marvin Carlson
THEOLOGY David F. Ford
THINKING AND REASONING
    Jonathan St B. T. Evans
THOMAS AQUINAS Fergus Kerr
THOUGHT Tim Bayne
TIBETAN BUDDHISM
    Matthew T. Kapstein
TIDES David George Bowers and
    Emyr Martyn Roberts
TOCQUEVILLE Harvey C. Mansfield
TOPOLOGY Richard Earl
TRAGEDY Adrian Poole
TRANSLATION Matthew Reynolds
THE TREATY OF VERSAILLES
    Michael S. Neiberg

TRIGONOMETRY Glen Van Brummelen
THE TROJAN WAR Eric H. Cline
TRUST Katherine Hawley
THE TUDORS John Guy
TWENTIETH-CENTURY BRITAIN
    Kenneth O. Morgan
TYPOGRAPHY Paul Luna
THE UNITED NATIONS
    Jussi M. Hanhimäki
UNIVERSITIES AND COLLEGES
    David Palfreyman and Paul Temple
THE U.S. CIVIL WAR Louis P. Masur
THE U.S. CONGRESS
    Donald A. Ritchie
THE U.S. CONSTITUTION
    David J. Bodenhamer
THE U.S. SUPREME COURT
    Linda Greenhouse
UTILITARIANISM
    Katarzyna de Lazari-Radek and
    Peter Singer
UTOPIANISM Lyman Tower Sargent
VETERINARY SCIENCE James Yeates
THE VIKINGS Julian D. Richards
VIRUSES Dorothy H. Crawford
VOLCANOES Michael J. Branney and
    Jan Zalasiewicz
VOLTAIRE Nicholas Cronk
WAR AND TECHNOLOGY
    Alex Roland
WATER John Finney
WAVES Mike Goldsmith
WEATHER Storm Dunlop
THE WELFARE STATE
    David Garland
WILLIAM SHAKESPEARE
    Stanley Wells
WITCHCRAFT Malcolm Gaskill
WITTGENSTEIN A. C. Grayling
WORK Stephen Fineman
WORLD MUSIC Philip Bohlman
THE WORLD TRADE
    ORGANIZATION Amrita Narlikar
WORLD WAR II Gerhard L. Weinberg
WRITING AND SCRIPT
    Andrew Robinson
ZIONISM Michael Stanislawski

Kenneth Le Meunier-FitzHugh

MARKETING

A Very Short Introduction

OXFORD
UNIVERSITY PRESS

OXFORD
UNIVERSITY PRESS

Great Clarendon Street, Oxford, OX2 6DP,
United Kingdom

Oxford University Press is a department of the University of Oxford.
It furthers the University's objective of excellence in research, scholarship,
and education by publishing worldwide. Oxford is a registered trade mark of
Oxford University Press in the UK and in certain other countries

First edition published in 2021

Impression: 1

Published in the United States of America by Oxford University Press
198 Madison Avenue, New York, NY 10016, United States of America

British Library Cataloguing in Publication Data
Data available

Library of Congress Control Number: 2020943420

ISBN 978-0-19-882733-7

Printed in Great Britain by
Ashford Colour Press Ltd, Gosport, Hampshire

Contents

Acknowledgements xvii

List of illustrations xix

1 The nature of marketing 1

2 Marketing research 16

3 Segmentation, targeting, and positioning, and the role of branding 30

4 Consumer and buyer behaviour and the value proposition 47

5 Promotions (marketing communications) and social media 63

6 Price and place (managing channels) 80

7 Product, new product development, and service marketing 97

8 The changing nature of marketing 114

References 131

Further reading 141

Index 145

Acknowledgements

I would like to note my gratitude to the colleagues who have helped in developing my understanding of the complexities of sales and marketing, specifically I would like to thank the late Nigel Piercy, David Jobber, and Nikala Lane. I am also grateful for the support of many friends and colleagues in the UK and the USA who have supported my work over the years. I also gratefully acknowledge the help and guidance provided by Heather de Lyon, who read the manuscript many times; and Jenny Nugee, the Editorial Team Leader for VSI series at OUP, and Andrea Keegan of OUP, all of whom have been very patient with me. However, my greatest vote of thanks must go to my wife, Leslie Caroline, who has had to listen to and read many iterations of my work over the years, and I should also mention that she has corrected my typing on many, many occasions.

List of illustrations

1 Pears' soap advert **5**
Photo by Hulton Archive /
Getty Images.

2 Customers' needs, wants,
and demands **9**

3 Expanded marketing mix **11**

4 Criteria for a viable
segment **32**

5 Positioning in relation to
segmentation and
targeting **42**

6 The buying decision-making
process **48**

7 Influences on purchasing
behaviours **51**

8 Influencers of buying
decisions **52**

9 Mailchimp value
proposition **59**
© Mailchimp®.

10 Key promotional
mix tools **65**

11 The communication
process **66**

12 Cadbury Gorilla advert **68**
Image Courtesy of The Advertising
Archives.

13 Consumer and B2B
promotions **71**

14 Megabus advertising **87**
Justin Kase zsixz / Alamy
Stock Photo.

15 Methods of distribution **93**

16 An example of multi-channel
distribution **94**

17 Constituents of a
product **99**

18 The BCC matrix or
Boston box **101**

19 The product lifecycle **103**

20 Marmite line extensions **105**
Peanut butter: Lenscap / Alamy Stock Photo; Marmite: Tim Gainey / Alamy Stock Photo.

21 The goods vs services continuum **110**

22 Key elements and marketing outcomes of AI **128**

Chapter 1
The nature of marketing

You will probably already have a good idea as to what you think marketing is about. After all, marketing is all around us and we are continuously bombarded by marketing messages at home, on our way to work, on holiday, and even when we are relaxing. We have discussions with friends about new advertisements and the latest promotions or products from our favourite brands. We are encouraged to write blogs and provide feedback to comparison sites. Our engagement with social media has moved us from being passive receivers of marketing messages to active participants, who share opinions, thoughts, and feelings about the things that we consume. However, even though marketing outputs are familiar to us, we should beware of dismissing marketing as an activity solely to 'make people buy' or 'just advertising'. Marketing encompasses much more than that, as it covers a wide range of essential business activities, to ensure that you can obtain the products and services that you want and need, when and how you want them.

Marketing has been described as about getting the 'right' product to the 'right' place with the 'right' promotion and at the 'right' price so that it will be purchased. However, a recent definition from the American Marketing Association suggests marketing is about communicating, delivering, and exchanging offerings that have value for customers, clients, partners, and society at large.

Leading marketer, Philip Kotler, explained that in a saturated marketplace it is more important than ever to anticipate and identify your customers' needs and wants, and to provide the value that satisfies them. Companies are desperately trying to stand out from the crowd, to grab our attention, and to gain our loyalty.

The function of marketing is fundamentally an exchange process based on the premise that—'I have something you want, and you have something I want, so let's do a deal!' The assumption is that each party will gain value from the exchange. The job of the marketer is to make sure that the customer is aware of what is being offered and that the offer will align with what they value most, whether this is a product, service, or an idea (a charity or good cause). Potential buyers should be willing to engage in the exchange by providing money and/or the time that is required. This mutual exchange of value should generate customer satisfaction and future repeat exchanges, creating customer loyalty and extending a mutually beneficial supplier/customer relationship.

Defining marketing

To understand some of the following discussions, we need to be clear about the difference between some key terms. Let us start with 'Goods' versus 'Service' and 'Customer' versus 'Consumer'. 'Goods' are physical products that can be made, configured (shaped), and transported to market. Examples might include fast-moving consumer goods (FMCG) such as packaged foods, toiletries, and beverages that sell rapidly at a relatively low price, or white and brown goods such as fridges, freezers, televisions, and audio equipment. A 'service' is an offer to the market that does not have a physical presence but provides value through interaction between the supplier and customer, such as consultancy, education, the leisure industry, and hairdressing. Services have been described as being intangible, perishable, variable, and inseparable from the provider. A haircut, gym class, or advice session has no independent physical existence, meaning it cannot be stored for later use. Each service event is perceived differently by the consumer and is inextricably linked to engagement with the supplier. One person's perfect haircut is another person's total disaster.

'Product' is often used (Including in this book) as an umbrella term for either a physical good or service, and is something that will provide value and/or satisfaction to its user or consumer in the marketplace. Many products purchased today will contain a combination of physical goods and service elements, and consequently lie somewhere between a physical 'good' and a 'service' offering. When going to a restaurant for a meal you receive the physical 'goods' of food and drinks, prepared by chefs and delivered to you by waiters that are the service elements. Some products offered for sale are mainly physical goods (table salt or a bicycle), but they are usually delivered to the purchaser through services such as a retail outlet or an online platform. Some product offers are nearer to pure service, for example osteopathy, insurance, or education. These service examples, such as accommodation in hotels, also have important physical aspects such as beds, facilities such as gym or swimming pool, and peripheral goods such as hotel toiletries.

There has been a lot of discussion about the differences between a customer and a consumer. The customer is the person that *purchases* the goods or services from the producer/supplier. The consumer is the person who actually *uses* the product or engages with the service provided. The customer may also be the consumer, but often the customer is an intermediary such as retail outlets, purchasers of raw materials, or franchise agents purchasing the right to use a brand name, for example, McDonald's franchisees. However, throughout this book, we intend to use the word customer to encompass both customers and consumers.

Where did marketing come from?

It has been argued that marketing is a concept that was developed from selling activities, as markets matured and competition between sellers of various products and services increased and there was a need for organizations to promote their offer in order to have the edge over their competitors. Organizations often divide sales and marketing into two separate functional areas with different personnel, responsibilities, and objectives. However, fundamentally, sales is a marketing activity and needs to be aligned with other marketing activities.

Marketing as a recognizable function today is believed to have started with advertising in pamphlets in the 1700s and it grew with the establishment of daily newspaper advertising in the early and mid-1800s. Billboard advertising became popular in the 1850s and this really started the serious promotional campaigns that were responsible for raising awareness of specific products and brands. An early example of successful marketing was the use of 'Bubbles' (see Figure 1) to sell Pears' soap in the late 19th century, which was initiated by Thomas James Barratt, the Chairman of A&F Pears (A&F Pears was later to be purchased by Lever Brothers, which is now the multinational Unilever). Considered to be the world's first brand marketer, Barratt used a range of promotional tools, including testimonials, slogans, images, sales promotions, and gifts, in order to boost sales of its distinctive soap products and also ensured that the product was widely available and competitively priced.

The next big step in marketing activities occurred in the 1950s, when TV advertising offered new media options with wider scope and more immediacy. Advertising is defined as the bought and paid-for communications that are delivered through various media such as TV, newspapers, and more recently online platforms. This development was followed in the early 1960s by

1. Pears' soap advert.

E. Jerome McCarthy's conceptualization of the marketing mix (Promotion, Price, Place, and Product), which has become the foundation of modern marketing strategy.

The scope of marketing

Marketing is divided into a number of different subsets or applications that are focused on reaching different groups in the marketplace. The most common applications are consumer marketing, business-to-business (B2B) marketing, service marketing, not-for-profit marketing, and international marketing. We are all consumers, which means that we use or experience the goods and services that we acquire. Consumer marketing (business-to-consumer—B2C) impinges on us every day in advertisements we see, direct mail (online and offline) and public relations messages we receive, sales promotions we engage with, and through pricing and delivery options for products.

B2B marketing is aimed at engaging organizations with products that help them carry out their operations. B2B purchases are ultimately driven by customer demand for these products. The range of products covered is wide-ranging and includes items such as raw materials, capital goods, office supplies, consultancies, and products for resale. B2B marketing takes a different form from consumer marketing (we further explore B2B marketing later in the volume). Service marketing is concerned with marketing an intangible product rather than a physical good and can be either B2B or B2C—for example, marketing airtime providers for mobile phones to both businesses and consumers. The standard marketing strategy of the four Ps (price, product, place, and promotion) is insufficient to cover the intangible elements of the offer which are expanded to include the additional Ps of people, physical product, and process (see section below for more detail). This extension to the marketing mix means that the different information required by service customers can be effectively communicated, such as the skills and expertise of the provider.

For example, a consultancy would market the skills and expertise of their *people*, have effective online *processes* for delivering the service, and provide certificates, invoices, or other *physical* documentation to support their brand.

International marketing requires a conceptual shift or change in focus from satisfying smaller, national markets to reaching global markets. To achieve this, organizations such as Toyota, Coca-Cola, and Unilever need to make adjustments to their marketing efforts to meet the needs of customers living with different cultures, language, legal conditions, and factor conditions (such as infrastructure, natural resources, and the environment they are operating within). The globalization of markets has been a major challenge because although global organizations have considerable choice on where to operate and where to sell, they have to adapt to various environmental and political situations and trading agreements in each territory.

Not-for-profit marketing is concerned with communicating the messages of those organizations that provide public goods and services, or those products that are produced for society's benefit, such as vaccines produced by pharmaceutical companies. In many cases public services are provided by government departments and include items such as health care, public transportation, the library service, education, and marketing campaigns aimed at changing society's behaviour, for example adverts for reducing the consumption of alcohol or smoking. Another form of not-for-profit marketing is designed for charities to help them raise funds for important causes, such as supporting an area that is experiencing famine, preventing cruelty to children and animals, or repairing historic buildings.

What is customer value?

Peter Doyle, leading academic of marketing, described value as a subjective element based on the participants' feelings and perceptions. Consequently, 'value' is a variable that is dependent on the point of view of the participants in the exchange. Value can take many forms, including a functional value (how the item can be used), monetary value (financial gain), social value (created in interaction), and psychological value (making people feel better). Customer-perceived value is based on the comparison of goods/services to similar products in the market. To offer value, marketers need to be aware of their customers' needs, wants, and demands, as well as being able to present their offer in the most beneficial way.

This focus on customer value has led to the development of the concept of co-creation of value, where the buyer and seller interact and cooperate to develop new products or find new uses for existing products. Value is created in the interaction between the two parties and can take many different forms, including knowledge exchange, identifying different uses for the product/service, increasing profitability/reducing costs, and creating a superior brand. The important part of co-creation of value is that it is developed through interactions between the parties, such as the buyer and seller. Architects, for example, will liaise with their customers when designing a building, so that additional value is created through the exchange of ideas and information.

Creating value through a market orientation

Competition within markets has increased exponentially over the past few decades. In response, many organizations have been adopting what is commonly called a market-orientated approach, which is where the organization as a whole focuses on meeting its customers' needs, allowing them to create greater customer value and satisfaction in order to attract and retain customers. An example of a market-orientated organization is the Apple Corporation, which is focused on delivering the best customer experience possible. Apple provide both goods and services in order to solve the challenges faced by society in communication and entertainment.

Apple are totally focused on their customers and delivering what they want. They have created interactive retail spaces where they can meet their customers and have provided website platforms that offer customer support and spaces for customer learning. Apple have developed new ranges of software applications to increase customer interaction with their products, as well as continuously innovating new products and reinventing existing ones to meet customer evolving needs. In this way Apple's market-orientation approach has increased sales and created intensely loyal customers.

Customers' needs, wants, and demands

It is necessary for organizations to understand their customers' needs, wants, and demands (see Figure 2). The needs of society are the most urgent elements and they relate to the things we need in order to survive and prosper. Consequently, businesses selling products that satisfy these needs are likely to experience consistent demand for their offer.

Needs	Satisfies a deprivation such as: Physical: food, clothing, warmth, and safety Social: belonging and affection Individual: knowledge and self-expression
Wants	Things that are desired but are not necessary to the individual's wellbeing. Wants are shaped by cultural and individual personality factors
Demands	Wants backed by buying power

2. Customers' needs, wants, and demands.

Needs include obtaining items essential for survival, such as food, clothing, and shelter, but once these basic needs have been met more intangible elements, such as feelings of belonging and affection or the individual's need for recognition and self-expression, become prominent. Wants are less urgent than needs, as they are driven by our desires and immediate concerns for satisfaction, which change with different situations, fashion, and over time. You may want a digital tablet for entertainment purposes, but you may need one to carry out your work more effectively. Demand is created by the cumulative ability of consumers to satisfy their needs and wants through engagement and purchasing of specific goods and services. Demand may also be generated through social concerns, like the growing demand for reduced sugar in food or employing models that are not all tall and size 0 but reflect the diversity in society. As a result, what customers want and demand change constantly. Keeping track of these changes is a primary function of marketing and is achieved through market research (see Chapter 2).

The marketing mix

Since the 1960s, marketing has used the four P's of Price (decisions concerning list pricing, discount pricing, and special offers), Place (the direct or indirect channels to market, where the products are sold), Product (which is what the business offers for sale), and Promotion (marketing communications, which includes advertising, public relations, direct selling, and sales promotions) to deliver its marketing objectives. A marketing mix for each customer group can be created by identifying how each element should be configured. However, the nature of marketing has changed in the last twenty years to include services and the traditional four Ps have been expanded to include another three Ps of People (the human interaction accompanying the service delivery), Physical Evidence (non-human elements of the service encounter, such as equipment, furniture, and facilities), and Process (sets of activities that result in the delivery of product benefits) (see Figure 3).

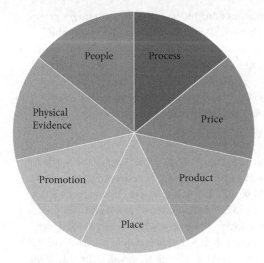

3. Expanded marketing mix.

Whatever type of product is being marketed, either services or goods, the function of marketing is to identify what each customer group wants and to develop a marketing mix that is built on the organization's strengths and conveys to the customer the value of what it is offering (see Chapter 3). These variables of the marketing mix may be combined in different ways to create the 'right' recipe for a certain target group. This recipe is predicated on the organization's understanding of the target markets' needs, wants, and demands.

The 'Product' part of the marketing mix is how the specification of the actual goods or service can be designed or adjusted so that they meet the customers' needs. Once the design for the generic product is set in place, the marketing team can configure the product to meet the needs of different target customers. This does not necessarily mean that the basic or core product's design is changed in substantial ways, but that the packaging and augmented features (such as warranties and colour availability) of

11

the product/service are adjusted to appeal to each target group. The brand name is a key part of the product element of the marketing mix, as it indicates the quality and value of the offer as a whole (see Chapter 5). The output of Heinz, a processed food manufacturer, is very similar to that of their competitors, but customers rely on the brand name of Heinz to indicate the superior quality and reliability of their products, which guides customers to make their selection.

The 'Place' (sometimes known as Channel) part of the marketing mix refers to how the product/service is delivered to the market. Marketing should be able to identify where customers expect to find these types of products and under which conditions they are willing to purchase them. Some products will be primarily sold through intermediaries such as retailers, while others may be sold directly to customers. Services are often provided directly from the supplier, for example Microsoft products. Although services may be purchased through an intermediary, customers will often have to engage with the provider to experience the service. For instance, the customer purchases access to Microsoft software, but has to go onto the Microsoft website to download the software. Therefore 'Place' includes all the various types of retail or wholesale situations, geographic regions, website platforms, or direct sales from which the item can be obtained (see Chapter 6).

'Promotions' (now frequently called marketing communications) covers all the ways in which the product is brought to the attention of potential customers, including advertising, sales promotions, public relations (PR), sponsorship, direct marketing (on- or offline), and personal selling (see Chapter 5). The development of website platforms has increased the opportunities for marketing to engage in promotions, but it is social media that has been the most transformational development for marketing promotions in terms of its effects on how the organization communicates online with potential customers. The development of mobile devices, such as Smartphones and tablets powered by fourth/fifth generation (4G/5G) technology, and widespread public Wi-Fi, have meant that a new and wholly flexible method of mass communication is available to all age groups. As a result, social media has changed 'promotions' forever, providing sellers with the opportunity to permanently and continuously alter customer expectations.

The 'Price' element of the marketing mix is the process of setting an appropriate price at which to market the product. The price should reflect the rarity and quality of the product being offered, but it cannot exceed what the market is willing to pay. This does not mean that marketers have total control over the price variable within the organization. Pricing for example, is likely to be influenced by many factors including the cost of production of goods and services. However, the marketing department is able to make adjustments within certain constraints, so that the price reflects the value proposition (see Chapter 4). Further the price of an offer does not only cover monetary aspects, but also the sacrifices, in terms of time and effort, required to obtain the desired items (see Chapter 6).

Marketing services

The growth of service offers, such as entertainment, banking, personal services, and transportation, has meant that the marketing mix has expanded to the seven Ps to include People, Physical Evidence, and Processes (see Figure 3). Marketing services is challenging, as there are many more variables involved in their delivery and greater variety in the perceived quality of the offer. When you go to the theatre to watch a new production you may have a very enjoyable experience, but the person next to you may not. This variation could be dependent on the individual's personal experience of obtaining the tickets and getting to the theatre (the process of attending), their interactions with the employees of the theatre, or even their prior knowledge/expectations of the skills of the actors (people), and their evaluation of the physical environment of the theatre and/or quality of the programme. This clearly indicates why the marketing mix has been extended to seven Ps, to cover the parts of the service offer that have a direct bearing on the customer's experience.

The difficulty is that these three extra Ps are less controllable than the original four Ps. The 'people' element will depend on many outside factors such as training, the attitude of the service provider, and the skills that they possess. The people delivering the service may not actually be part of the selling organization, as they may be employed by an intermediary or even outsourced. 'Processes' (including customer service) are also variable depending on the nature of the service, time constraints, level of organizational skills, information technology (IT) facilities, and other resources available to the providing organization. The physical evidence (environment, quality of the website, and documentation) provided may also impact on the perceived value of the service, as it may be considered excellent by some customers, but only average by others. To take Apple as an example, they recruit their retail employees (people) carefully, and provide ongoing and continuous training and an excellent set of organizational values by which to operate. They also carefully control the physical selling environment around the world (physical evidence) and provide excellent technical support for their products. Finally, their processes are very well organized, providing a seamless delivery of their products and services to customers with excellent back-up systems (processes).

The marketing mix for services can be configured to meet the needs of different groups within a single market, for example British Airways provides different marketing strategies for different target groups. The service to the economy passengers includes the same secure and efficient transportation that is offered to business and first-class passengers, as they are on the same plane. However, the *price* element is very different, and the *people* element is also different due to the level of service offered in each cabin. The *process* is more interactive in first-class, and the *physical* elements of seating and food for business and first-class passengers are superior to those offered to the economy passengers.

Marketing needs to be customer centric, as its objective is to meet customers' needs and provide superior value in order to create competitive advantage. This value should be delivered in a beneficial way for both the organization and the customer. The organization 'promises' in its communications that the goods/service will delight the recipient in some way and the whole of the organization's capabilities should aim to deliver on these promises. An organization's capabilities are a combination of the skills and processes they employ to create the product or services for which the organization is known. Companies are not equally good at all things and will have various strengths and weaknesses. Inevitably there are some areas where compromises have to be made, but overall the most successful companies are those that use their strengths and capabilities to deliver an offer that best meets the needs of their customers. Marketing has the responsibility of identifying its customer requirements through market research and for developing a strategy that communicates the final value of its offer to the marketplace, thereby creating customer loyalty.

Chapter 2
Marketing research

Marketing research is one of the most engaging parts of marketing, as it is the opportunity for organizations to evaluate marketing performance, uncover customer behaviours, and explore their preferences. Good marketing research is the foundation of marketing strategy and it needs to be carried out rigorously and almost continuously, because customers' needs are continually changing, sometimes rapidly or in a major way, and at other times subtly or in small ways. Market research is about investigating markets rather than customers and has a broader scope than marketing research, in that it explores areas such as changes in the business environment, market structure, and trends through market analysis. Both marketing research and market research are carried out for reasons other than just to sell more products. Governments and industries use market/marketing research to find out what society wants, needs, and demands, so that they can write manifestos or put funds into certain types of research and development (R&D). We will concentrate on marketing research, as to be successful, the marketer relies heavily on up-to-date information specifically about customers' behaviours, competitors, and market trends.

Marketing research is described as the systematic gathering, recording, and analysis of data, and The American Marketing Association provides the following definition of its purpose:

Marketing research is the function that links the consumer, customer, and public to the marketer through information—information used to identify and define marketing opportunities and problems; generate, refine, and evaluate marketing actions; monitor marketing performance; and improve understanding of marketing as a process. Marketing research specifies the information required to address these issues, designs the method for collecting information, manages and implements the data collection process, analyses the results, and communicates the findings and their implications.

Marketing research looks beyond the immediate target market to provide information on changes in society as a whole, customer trends, and competitor developments to provide marketing planning guidance, and to identify future opportunities and threats in the marketplace. The industry operates globally and, according to ESOMAR's report, global marketing research alone was worth US$47 billion in 2018.

Marketing research covers a range of activities which may be positioned as either problem-identification research or problem-solving research. The problem-identification research will seek to uncover why something is happening or find new opportunities. For example, an organization may wish to uncover why there has been a change in customers' attitudes towards their brand, or why groups of customers have changed their purchasing behaviours, or if a new group of customers are interested in the organization's product. For example, trainers are now being sold as high fashion items and gaining a whole new customer base. Problem-solving research helps you to work out how to address the issues uncovered in problem identification. If a group of customers has changed their purchasing behaviours due to a change of price, you would want to find out what the new price point is at which you would be able to sell your product. It is very hard to plan an effective marketing strategy without marketing research. Consequently, there is a need to carry out marketing research at differing levels to identify local, national, regional, and

Table 1. Purpose of different types of marketing research

Advertising research	Including copy testing of text, gauging customers' response, brand awareness and organizational visibility.
Brand association	Identifying what customers associate with certain brand names and what they understand are the brands' values.
Buyer decision-making	Determining what motivates people to buy, what is involved in the process, and what are the buying triggers.
Concept testing	Testing the reaction of customers to a particular concept or new product offering.
Trend spotting	Identifying changes in cultural trends and new trends in buyer behaviours.
Customer satisfaction	Identifying what constitutes satisfaction in a range of customer groups/segments and markets.
Demand forecasting	Estimating the approximate total level of demand for a specific product or product group.
Distribution trends	Investigating the attitude of retailers and associated distributors towards certain brands/products and how they should be conveyed to the marketplace.
Internet intelligence	Searching for customers' opinions and trends via chatrooms, web pages, blogs, etc., and following opinion formers.
Marketing analytics and effectiveness	Building scenario models and measuring the results of theoretical marketing actions.
Mystery shopping	The anonymous gathering of data on the customers' interaction with the product or distribution. Often used for quality control.
Market positioning	Positioning research is used to identify the brand/product's position in the market compared to other offers.
Price elasticity	To determine how price sensitive a particular product/product group is to changes in price.

Sales forecasting	Carried out to predict the possible sales based on estimates of demand and the influence of other factors including advertising campaigns.
Segmentation identification	Determining the key characteristics of various groups of buyers.
Online panels	Groups of individuals who are asked to consider various aspects of the organization's offer and marketing activities.
Store audits	Reviewing the sales of certain products or groups of products to identify the potential market share or product turnover.
Test marketing	A small-scale launch of a new product line to estimate the market/customers' response.

global customer trends, so that marketing planning can anticipate changes to customers' needs that are difficult to identify in any other way.

This list of potential marketing research activities shown in Table 1 is not exhaustive, but it demonstrates the range of activities carried out by marketers.

Sources of data and information

The issue with marketing research is not *finding* information to analyse, as the world is bursting with information from thousands of different sources. The real challenge is to find the *right* information from both inside and outside the organization, so providing marketing intelligence and customer insights. Management information systems (MISs) are built around the decision-making needs of managers as they are designed to provide up-to-date information about the organization's operations. Internal data comes from the organization's own records of sales, customer activities, accounts, production figures, and costings. This data is specific to the organization and is therefore not replicable by other businesses and could provide valuable customer insights. MIS provides data that is continuously updated automatically from internal sources.

Secondary or *desk research* is carried out through interrogating existing sources of information from external sources. Secondary data can be collected from many different sources such as marketing reports, government statistics on demographics (changes in population figures such as age groups, gender, income levels, and ethnicity), and economic performance, and the penetration and take up of the internet in various regions. Data from secondary research is used to provide background information about the market, competitors' activities, and customer insights from a range of different perspectives. The advantages of using this type of data are that it is usually less expensive than primary research to collect, it is readily available, and it has already been analysed. Market analysts will produce reports about various industries and market sectors as required and provide reports that are generally available.

Primary or *field data* is collected by the researcher for specific research projects and is critical in enabling the organization to identify specific changes in the marketplace. The advantage of primary research is that it is carried out by your organization (or on your behalf). The data will be original and designed to provide information to answer your questions or solve specific problems. The main disadvantage of primary research is that if the research plan is not robust, the market information derived may be biased and lead to poor decision-making. Additionally, primary research is costly to carry out and analyse. In most scenarios, marketing research is carried out through a combination of secondary and primary research, so that the findings from each source can be supported and confirmed through cross-referencing the information.

Quantitative data is collected from questionnaires and large data sets. It is number-based data that may be subject to statistical analysis and is considered to provide verifiable (repeatable) information. We rely on the findings from quantitative-based research to shape our understanding of the world and provide marketers with relevant, accurate, reliable, and valid information. Most governments will provide quantitative information about the demographics of their country, size of population, how it is divided into sectors, including by age group, ethnicity, geographical spread, income levels, and religious groups. Organizations collect quantitative data for a number of purposes, including identifying market trends, target groups, strengths and weaknesses of products, usability of websites, and behaviour patterns.

Qualitative data is opinion-based and is used to increase our understanding of why things happen. Specifically, researchers collect qualitative data to find out why customers buy certain products, select one brand over another, and what they think about the products they purchase. You should note that findings from qualitative-based data can be open to greater interpretation than those from quantitative data, as it focuses on feelings and emotions that can be considered subjective. Qualitative data is usually collected from a small number of respondents and may not be generalizable to the whole population, but it provides insights that are useful to organizations in their decision-making processes. These two types of data provide different types of marketing information and can be described as answering 'what, why, and how' marketing questions.

Research methods

There are many ways of carrying out primary research. One of the most common methods is through a survey. A survey is a standardized way of collecting data from a selected group of respondents (a sample), so that information and insights can be gained on topics of interest. As surveys are carried out for a variety of purposes, different methods can be used depending on the objective of the research. Surveys are designed to collect information through a questionnaire that is completed by relevant respondents, with the necessary experience. Consequently, care needs to be taken to ensure that the right people are targeted, and the right questions are asked to avoid bias or creating misinformation. Questionnaires provide data that can be tested and measured. However, there is a trend to include some qualitative questions in questionnaires to provide greater depth of understanding. Questionnaires can be delivered remotely, through the post or via emails and social media, or more personally on the telephone or face-to-face.

To collect qualitative data, focus groups and interviews can be employed. A focus group is where a representative group of potential customers (between six and twelve people) are selected to represent the target customer. This group is then presented with something to evaluate: a product, a concept, or a problem. Questions are posed to the group, and their discussions and reactions are recorded. The difficulty with focus groups is that their responses may be influenced by the knowledge they are being observed and/or they may know what the purpose of the focus group is, so participants may change their reactions to provide the results they think the researcher wants. A good example would be Unilever providing taste tests for one of its key products/brands—Marmite. They assembled two groups of target customers from a new market, India. They provided one group with samples of Marmite spread on toast and recorded the group's responses. The results were uniformly negative as the taste was too strong. However, they gave the second group an everyday curry dish with Marmite added as a flavouring. This was much more positively received, as Marmite added a nice tang to the dish and was perceived as healthy, as it included vitamin B12 and other benefits to their diet.

Interviews are personalized interactions with a researcher that may be guided by a set of semi-structured questions, which provide more focused information about motivations and reactions. Interviews provide the opportunity for answers to be explored in greater depth. By asking follow-up questions the interviewer is able to gain clarity and understanding of respondents' views. However, interviews can only be carried out with a limited number of people as they are time-consuming to conduct and analyse.

Two other types of marketing research are experiments and observation. Observations (ethnographic studies) take place without interference from the researcher and happen without the participants being aware of the observation (as far as possible), for example recording customers' purchasing behaviours, monitoring TV viewing, or tracking customers' movements around a retail environment. Observations may raise issues of breaching privacy and permission may have to be obtained to use the data from the observation. The advantage of observations is that the customer's interactions with the product are not conditioned or influenced by the researcher or the environment. However, how the observation is set up is critical in achieving objectivity. Observers will need to be carefully briefed about why the observation is taking place, what to record, and what to ignore. If it is unstructured, then the observer should note or record everything that is happening within the observation area, as many factors could influence the customer's behaviour. Mystery shopping is an example of an observation and is where organizations employ someone to purchase products, sample services, and record their experiences. The aim is for them to observe customer service, ask questions, and even make complaints. The key is that the mystery shopper is anonymous and has the same experience as all other shoppers. Mystery shopping is often used to gain information about how a product is perceived in the retail environment and for quality control.

Experiments are basically observations that occur under controlled conditions. Experiments are set up so that conditions can be changed to enable specific outcomes and reactions to be recorded. The subjects are aware that they are taking part in research and they may be given some idea as to why the research is taking place. You may have been asked to take part in some experimental research, such as being presented with two or three different 'brand stories' and being asked which one you prefer and why. Participants can also be allocated to participate in different experimental conditions (different people to each condition, or the same person experiencing all conditions) and their reactions compared and recorded.

One of the newer methods of marketing research aimed at understanding customers' perceptions of brands and advertising is neuromarketing. This is where the researcher records brain scans that measure neural activity in response to different images and stimuli. Tracking of eye movement, eye dilation, and facial expressions (including heart and respiration rates) provides measurable insights into customer responses to changes in product design and marketing. The potential benefits of neuromarketing include more effective marketing campaigns and fewer product/campaign failures.

Marketing research is time-consuming to set up and has to be carefully recorded, so that subsequent researchers can reproduce the process in future and compare results. An example of an observation would be to watch and record the flow of customers around a retail space so that the presentation of products can be improved.

Sampling

Sampling is widely used in primary research. The purpose of sampling is to remove the need to ask every member of the target customer group (population) to respond to the survey. Sampling is the selection of a small group of people from the whole population (sampling frame) to represent the group. The aim is to ensure that the sample survey accurately reflects views that are in line with those of the whole population. Choosing the sample is challenging as it is easy to have a selection bias, which is where one part of the population is either over- or underrepresented. To avoid selection bias, the researcher may employ a probability sampling method, such as stratified sampling where the sample is selected to match the characteristics of the population. Therefore, if the whole population is made up of 30 per cent males, 70 per cent females, with 5 per cent under 20 years of age, 40 per cent between 21 and 40 years, 35 per cent 41 to 60, and 20 per cent over 61, then the sample should have people selected in those proportions to accurately represent that population. Alternatively, researchers may select a simple random sample, where every member of the population has an equal opportunity to be included in the sample but participants are selected totally randomly.

There are also non-probability sampling methods that are available to the researcher, such as quota samples or convenience samples, which may be used depending on the purpose or objective of the survey and the barriers to reaching suitable respondents (see Table 2). The sampling technique saves marketers a considerable amount of time and money, but it does open up the risk of a sample being either too small to be useful, or too skewed to one view or another by a poor sampling method that compromises its accuracy or validity.

The marketing research process

Research should have explicit objectives and be carefully planned. Many organizations will begin with a research statement that defines the potential problem and scope of the research. They will then consider the context that the research is taking place within, to identify the environmental conditions that may impact on the research. The third step would be to explore the nature of the problem, for example if the information required needs to be qualitative or quantitative, and then to carry out an investigation into who could provide this information. Defining the relationships between the variables may also be helpful to identify what is

Table 2. Sampling methods

Probability sample—all elements will have a chance to be included in the sample	
Simple random sample	Every member of the population has a known and equal chance of selection.
Stratified random sample	The population is divided into mutually exclusive groups and samples are drawn randomly from each group.
Cluster (area) sample	The population is divided into mutually exclusive groups and the researcher draws a random sample from one or more accessible groups.

Non-probability sample—the sample is selected from a restricted number of elements	
Snowball sample	The researcher selects a suitable respondent, interviews them and asks them for recommendations of other possible respondents in their network.
Judgemental or purposive sample	The researcher uses their judgement to select population members who in their opinion have information on the topic under research.
Quota sample	The researcher finds and interviews a prescribed number of people in each of several categories, for example 40% female and 60% male. The researcher stops interviewing females when the 40% quota is reached but continues to interview males until the 60% quota is reached.

likely to impact upon what and under which conditions. The final step would be to discuss the implications and costs of different courses of action, to identify how the research could be most effectively carried out.

It is crucial to ensure that your marketing strategy is based on a clear understanding of your customers and the identification of competitors' actions. The marketing research plan will provide a structured approach to identifying market needs and trends, customer insights, and competitors' strategies. By providing these kinds of additional insights, the marketing research plan will help to identify how to position a product to win in the market, something which is pivotal to the success of the business.

Customer insights and big data

In order for marketers to create value for their customers they need to develop accurate customer information, which is usually called customer insights. Detailed customer insights ensure that individual organizations within an industry are able to create competitive advantage. According to management guru Michael Porter, competitive advantage can be created either through differentiating the product (so that it is a distinctive offer to the market), or by providing the offer at the lowest cost (price advantage). As the majority of organizations within an industry cannot trade at the lowest price point (this market position can only be held by a single company), most organizations will compete through some form of differentiation, or a combination of low cost and differentiation. You could argue that in the mobile phone market the main competitors have differentiated themselves by offering things that their customer insights have identified as being valued by the target customer. Apple, for example, provides a 'full-service' offer of integrated hardware and software, while Samsung offers more features on their phones that are technically advanced. Huawei competes on value for money (more features at a lower price point) and Sony on innovative design and R&D. Each offer meets the needs/wants of a different section of the market and relies on customer insights to make sure that they emphasize the right aspects of the offer for each target group.

The ability to gather customer information digitally and via social media has given rise to the development of 'big data' analytics. Big data is continuously being collected as customers interact with organizations and it provides a new source of customer insights, which enable marketers to adjust their strategies and provide more personalized communications/offers. If the analysis of digital customer data indicates that, for example, 40 per cent of females in the 35–45 age bracket indicated that 'green issues' were of concern, or that 64 per cent of males aged between 25 and 35 would prefer to pay for 'large ticket items in instalments', the marketers are able to adjust their communications to emphasize the organization's 'green' credentials or to offer payment-by-instalment facilities. Analysing big data sets is also opening up internal sources of data that used to be closed to marketers because the data sets were too large and complex to access.

Analysing data

Once the data has been collected it needs to be analysed to turn it into useable marketing intelligence that will hopefully answer the key questions about what is happening in the market. In simple terms, analysing data involves examining it to reveal repeated patterns, trends, relationships, consistency, or frequency. When analysing qualitative data, you are looking for how frequently certain words or actions are occurring and to establish consistency in reported behaviours (when the same responses are being repeated by different respondents). Researchers will also look for new understandings that explain behaviours and changes in the market. An example may be mobile phone companies using quantitative data to identify that customers are using their phones more for activities unrelated to making calls (such as searching for information, entertainment, and to shop online), but they analyse qualitative data to explain why and how this is happening.

Quantitative data offers options for different types of analysis. At a simple level, graphs can be used to describe the shape of the overall data and visually present trends and quantities to bring out the key points. Relationships can be analysed through a number of different tests, including correlations (which explore relationships between variables). For example, a correlation may be run to see if the number of hours of sunshine correlates with the amount of ice cream purchased.

When marketing research can go wrong

In the 1980s, Coca-Cola carried out extensive marketing research into their consumers' preferences and attitudes to their cola offer by carrying out consumer taste tests, surveys, and retail-based interviews. They concluded that their existing product was being outperformed by the Pepsi product in terms of taste. They carried out research to find out what their customers wanted from a potential new product, before they launched their 'New Coke'. They created a new look to the packaging and one of the most extensive US marketing campaigns ever seen. However, when the product was launched it was a huge failure. What the marketing research had not captured was that Coca-Cola's customers had a huge investment in the tradition and heritage of the existing product, which the organization had been promoting for nearly a hundred years. Changing the taste and look of Coca-Cola was simply not acceptable to their home consumers, despite the 'improved' taste and a massive marketing campaign. The marketing research had not been inaccurate, but how the market information was interpreted led to a series of disastrous marketing decisions. Marketing research is vital in helping organizations to get closer to meeting their customers' needs, but it should be carried out cautiously, bearing in mind the possible pitfalls.

Chapter 3

Segmentation, targeting, and positioning, and the role of branding

Can you sell your products and services universally to the whole market and all customers? For some products, particularly commodities such as mains water, fruit, vegetables, and salt, you can, and you should. However, the majority of organizations recognize that they are unable to appeal to every buyer in the same way, or even every buyer of that product group. Customers come in all shapes and sizes, with different motivations and desires, and consequently it is possible to identify defined customer groups and design marketing strategies that are relevant to those groups. This is called segmenting and targeting the market. Some products, such as cola and banking services, can be mass marketed to many different markets in a similar way, with only minor changes needed to the marketing mix to make the offer suitable for different customer groups. For example, Tesco will appeal to a number of different customer segments by offering different product ranges such as 'Everyday Value' for cost conscious customers, branded products (such as Heinz tinned products or Kenco coffee) for the loyal customers, and Tesco finest range that is targeted at customers seeking food for special occasions. Consequently, many products ranges can be more effectively marketed if the mix is targeted to meet the needs of distinctive customer segments. However, it is important to remember when carrying out a segmentation exercise that it is your customers or clients that you are segmenting, not the product groups.

Philip Kotler, marketing guru, highlighted that it is not possible to know what the ideal segmentation method will be for each individual business or industry, but there are usually general or broad segments that will be appropriate to most businesses such as demographic, geographic, or behavioural segmentations. For example, in the clothing industry an initial segmentation is likely to be between male and female customers, followed by segmentation by age (of both demographic factors). Consequently, suppliers could focus on male, female, or children's clothing, and become experts and recognized for supplying one of these groups. Although the British retailer Marks & Spencer provides men's and ladies' fashion and children's clothes, their reputation is, in reality, built on ladies' fashion, which is one of their core segments. Another segmentation could be by behaviour, for example clothing for specific activities, such as leisure, sport, business, or for celebrations. Once an organization has completed their segmentation exercise, they will then be able to select the segments in which they will be most successful because they have the skills and resources to provide a competitive offer.

We will also consider within this chapter the importance of creating brands that distinguish a business or product group in the marketplace from its competitors and recognize its overall value to the organization. A brand is an intangible asset of the organization that embodies the values the business stands for, because their brand name is supported by their reputation, for instance Chanel or Aviva. However, it is not only organizations that can create a brand, as both individual products or product groups and individuals such as Lady Gaga can have their own brand-personalized image. There is a lot of hype around establishing a strong brand name and image, as there seems to be a belief that without a strong brand a product has no market presence and therefore will not be able to differentiate itself from its competitors or form attachments with its customers. Of course, there are many famous brands that have differentiated themselves very successfully. Apple and Coca-Cola are two of the most successful, brand-led organizations, but there are many products that are successfully sold without a large brand presence, such as generic clothing or milk (although, even this is now marketed as 'own brand' in supermarkets or specialist marketplaces). We will explore what a brand is and how brands can be created, as well as considering the links between branding and segmentation.

What is segmentation?

The overall purpose of segmentation is to ensure that the organization's resources are directed at segments that are going to provide the best returns, as each of the identified segments can then be targeted with tailored marketing campaigns that optimize sales. However, each segment must meet specific criteria. It must be possible to differentiate the needs of one segment from another and to measure its size. For a segment to be viable it must be large enough to be profitable and it must be possible to communicate with the segment to be able to persuade those within it to adopt a product offer. If these criteria can be met, then the identified segment is likely to be profitable. Creating a new marketing mix for each newly identified segment is costly, and so care should be taken with selecting the segmentation criteria (see Figure 4). It would not be commercially viable to create a marketing mix for every new segment if there are not substantial differences between groups, or if the existing marketing mix is already working effectively.

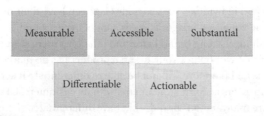

4. Criteria for a viable segment.

New segments can be identified where there are gaps in the market that can be exploited. The car industry has identified twenty-one definable segments in Europe, such as family cars, two-seater sports cars, and small SUVs. However, many major car manufacturers choose not to compete in every segment and only select those in which they can compete most effectively. Jaguar/Land Rover and Porsche for example primarily target premium segments, but further subdivide this premium segment into offers for single men/women, family drivers, the super wealthy, and business executives. Each organization targets these specific groups with a different marketing mix, including different features and benefits that will meet the target segment's needs. Mercedes-Benz and the other German car manufacturers Audi and BMW have successfully targeted a younger audience by created a marketing mix and new product offer that does not undermine their premium brand value but appeals to millennial and generation X drivers. To understand how this can be done, accurate information from marketing research is essential to identify their exact requirements.

Methods of segmentation

There is no single way to segment a market in a particular industry. Marketers will test various segmentation methods, and use them in different combinations, until they find the combination that provides the best segments for them. That being said, there are four generic segmentation methods that are commonly used to group customers by their overall characteristics: geographic, demographic (sometimes called profiling), psychographic, and behavioural (see Table 3).

We have already mentioned some of the demographic segmentation criteria, including those that are related to gender and age. To these two characteristics, we can add income brackets and customers' life-stage, such as teenage, young family, empty nesters, or pensioners. Marketers should beware of too much generalization, as

Table 3. Segmentation characteristics in consumer product

Segmentation variable	Examples
Demographic (profile)	
Age and gender	Male/female/transgender; and age groups, e.g. 18–21, 22–30, etc.
Lifecycle position	Single, early career, new couples, growing family, middle-aged, pensioners
Social class	Unemployed, unskilled working, skilled working, clerical, professional
Education	To 16 years, degree, post-graduate degree, professional qualifications
Income bracket (per annum)	Under £20,000, £21,000–£35,000, £36,000–£50,000, over £51,000
Geographic	
Location	Continent, country, region, urban vs rural
Geodemographic	Predominant housing such as rental; home ownership of apartments, small houses, detached housing
Behavioural	
Benefits sought	Convenience, quality, status, performance
Purchasing occasion or habit	Self-buy, repeated purchase, gift, brand switching
Usage	Frequent use, specialist use, occasional use
Perceptions and belief	Reputation, meets requirements, satisfaction
Psychographic	
Lifestyle	Trendsetter, conservative, innovator, settled, designer
Self-image	Experimenter, sophisticated, leader, adventurous
Personality	Extrovert, introvert, assertive, easily led

the segment of pensioners, for example, can include a wide variety of wants and needs, including those that are interested in international travel, those still in full-time work, and those with time-consuming hobbies. If it is necessary to divide the market more finely, other demographic segmentations can be employed, including education, ethnicity, occupation, religion, or family size.

Geographic segmentation is employed when it is important to take different cultural and environmental conditions into account to provide the best offer to the market. The geographical segmentation can be quite broad, considering continents or regions, or restricted to countries, districts, or towns. It is also possible to group geographical segments by those with common needs and wants, for example a clothing organization may segment on weather conditions and target all temperate territories, or Gucci may target countries that value Italian style such as Japan, China, or the United States.

Psychographic segmentation considers the elements of social class, personality, and lifestyle to help select groups of customers with similar needs. The criteria selected will depend on the industry and competitive positioning of the product being marketed, but overall the aim is to identify what is important to how that customer group lives. An example is the growing trend to become more environmentally friendly, which is driving an increase in demand for car rentals and car sharing rather than car ownership, presenting an opportunity to create new offers to suppliers of transportation, particularly in cities. The relevant segment characteristics are customers that are aware and engaged in debates on how to become more ethical and 'green', but also have the ability to pay for differentiated offers. This target segment provides a new opportunity for many different industries including food, clothing, building, and of course transportation.

Travel companies have long segmented their customers by their personality traits, including adventure seekers, or those requiring a high level of comfort, customers needing entertainment laid on, or those that prefer to be more ad hoc in what they do on holiday. Marketers have also segmented on brand values and identified psychographic segments, which are sometimes called brand tribes, who are interested in anything that is associated with that particular brand. McDonald's have their own followers, as do Nike and Lacoste, and these customers will not consider offers from competitors. In the mobile phone market, Apple, Samsung, and Huawei each have their own brand tribes. There is an interesting piece of research carried out on how populations might respond to disaster planning, by Kate Daellenback, Joy Parkinson, and Jayne Krisjanous, which revealed that there are four broad segments: (a) the 'unprepared and uninterested' who will only engage with disaster planning if encouraged/forced to by external influencers; (b) the 'it's just too difficult' group who are aware of the need, but will only engaged if barriers are lowered; (c) the 'willing but could do more' group, who will respond to targeted messages, but will not be proactive; and (d) the 'knowing, interested and prepared' group that will spread the word and help with preparation. The identification of these segments and their characteristics will help planners to gain a faster and more positive response from the population threatened with a disaster.

If psychographic segments use personality features, then behavioural segmentation uses the customers' responses to a product to segment the market in a different way. Behavioural segmentation is a powerful tool as it seeks to divide customers into groups based on the benefits sought, usage, and status conferred by using a product. Some behavioural segmentations are based on specific occasions, such as different weather, seasons, holidays, or celebrations. Certain products are associated with the winter season, including soup, warm clothing, products for dealing with ice, or road gritting, while others are associated with special occasions such as Chinese New Year, Christmas, birthdays, or anniversaries.

Another very popular type of behavioural segmentation method, linked to brand tribes, is loyalty. Many organizations have created a loyal following by offering membership cards that confer benefits, such as free gifts, on the loyal customer. The market can be behaviourally segmented, and many airlines have employed loyalty segmentation. British Airways, for example, have subdivided their customers by frequency of use. Bronze, Silver, and Gold loyalty cards are conferred on members depending on how frequently and far they travel. They provide different benefits for each group in the hope of enticing the customer to move into the next group up by displaying greater loyalty.

Most marketers use multiple segmentation methods to try to identify and target new, better-focused segments that have the potential to be very profitable. An example of multi-level segmentation comes from the clothing industry. The initial segmentation could be on geographical factors, as different regions have various climatic conditions and cultures that broadly affect clothing usage. Demographics could then further segment the market by gender, age, and income. The next level of segmentation could be on behavioural characteristics, for example what the clothes are going to be used for; and a further level could be psychographic, by identifying personality or lifestyle traits that would attract you to certain styles of clothing. Each organization in the clothing industry will carry out their own segmentation exercise to identify the key segments that are appropriate to their own strengths and resources, so they can design a marketing strategy to successfully target each individual segment, such as Christian Dior or Givenchy meeting the needs of haute couture customers, compared to Burberry or Barbour targeting customers more interested in country-style clothing.

Business-to-business segmentation

In B2B marketing, segmentation techniques are applied differently from those used for consumer markets. B2B markets are characterized by a relatively small number of customers who are purchasing for their own use, for resale, or to incorporate the item into another product. Whatever the case, B2B buyers are purchasing on behalf of an organization rather than an individual customer, and therefore the psychographic and demographic variables are not appropriate. Importantly, B2B purchasing decisions are not usually made by a single person or a small family, but by a formal decision-making unit (see Chapter 4), which is made up of participants who are stakeholders in the decision and are experts in their field. It has been argued that B2B buyers are more rational because they are not personally invested in the decision and B2B products can be more complex.

The broad characteristics that are commonly used to segment B2B markets are based on the characteristics of the organizations (sometimes called macro segmentations) and their purchasing behaviours (sometimes called micro segmentations). Marketers can adopt three types of organizational characteristics to broadly segment the market: geographic, industry type, and company size. Using geographical location characteristics to segment allows the marketing mix to be configured to meet regional variations in purchasing practice and price built on the assumption that countries that are in close proximity will have many common traits, needs, and behaviours. However, some countries in close proximity could vary greatly in fundamental aspects such as culture, language, and economics. Many countries in Europe display these differences, so that buying requirements and behaviours in Germany, for example, are likely to be quite different from those in France or Spain. Basic geographical segmentation should consequently be supplemented by the cultural and economic factors, which could result in South American operations being grouped with some of those in Southern Europe with which they share similarities (e.g. language and history).

Basing the segmentation of the market by industry type has clear benefits because each industry is formed to meet a specific customer need, such as sports equipment for gyms, or companies that cater for business travel. The requirements of the buyer of sports equipment will align with the needs of other purchasers of the same type of business products. These similarities can be used to configure offers for each segment. Using industry segmentation is useful as an initial division of the market, but it may be necessary to segment the market further on product type or product usage. For example, within the sports equipment industry suppliers may have different marketing mixes for sports centre buyers to those for buyers from hotels' leisure centres.

Using organization size as the basis of the segmentation will allow the marketer to adapt their marketing to the formalized purchasing processes of large organizations or chains operating from multiple locations, in comparison to the more informal purchasing behaviours of smaller organizations. In addition to these basic segmentations by size some organizations will need to cater for the individual needs of super-large or multinational enterprises (MNEs), because these customers will require a customized approach as they are purchasing expensive and complex products, or purchasing in very large quantities (even, potentially, the supplier's entire stock of a particular product), for example in the case of steel for manufacturing cars and other vehicles.

When the broad segmentation of B2B markets is insufficient to identify clear segments with definable needs, it is possible to supplement with micro segmentation criteria. The most frequent way to micro segment B2B buyers would be through a combination of benefits sought, purchasing behaviours, and customer personality, as these characteristics condition how the marketer approaches the customer. To produce recognizable segments based on these micro segmentation criteria some organizations will give each one a distinctive name, such as conservative followers (those who maintain the existing relationships with their suppliers), opportunists (who will negotiate with a range of sellers to gain temporary advantage), or evaluators (who regularly review their suppliers for efficiency and quality). The two-stage approach to segmentation, macro and micro, has been developed to manage the complexity of having to respond to the combination of organizational and individualistic decision-making processes that exists in B2B markets.

Targeting

Targeted marketing is about selecting the segments that offer the greatest potential for profit and developing a tactical marketing strategy for each group. Jean Paul Gaultier has developed two perfumes that are clearly targeted at different segments, one for males (Le Male) and the other for females (Classique). The marketing mix for each of these products has been designed to appeal to a specific segment. The bottle shape is either male or female, and the contents has an appropriate fragrance, so the targeting is focused on delivering two clear value propositions. However, their research identified that young couples were an unserved segment, so although Gaultier is selling two products they are actually targeting one segment: young couples. The pricing, distribution, and advertising are joint, as the two products are priced, promoted, and displayed together, making the two products a double purchase.

The four types of targeting strategies are undifferentiated, differentiated, focused, and customized (i.e. mostly used in B2B marketing). Undifferentiated marketing is when the marketing campaign targets the whole market and the campaign is focused on meeting the common needs of all their customers. A good example of undifferentiated marketing is the world-wide marketing campaign for Coca-Cola. The product is presented to every market and every segment in the same way. It is distributed through multi channels (anywhere people may require soft drinks), in single containers, six packs, large bottles, or through a pump. The pricing structure is very similar in all markets with any variations being driven by local economic conditions. The promotional messages ('an enjoyable way to quench your thirst'), logos, and stories are the same around the world.

Differentiated marketing campaigns are designed to sell the product in a way that appeals to each of the identified target segments. The duplication of marketing effort obviously creates higher marketing costs than undifferentiated or focused marketing, but should yield higher revenues and greater profits overall. A good example of differentiated offers comes from the car industry. Ford manufactures a range of cars based on a generic platform. The Ford Fiesta and Eco-Sport are designed to meet the needs of two different customer segments. The Fiesta is targeted at the single, younger driver or at young families, while the Eco-Sport targets the lifestyle of the 'urban jungle' customer, by offering greater ground clearance and a 'pumped-up' look. Some organizations adopt a focused strategy for their product offer. For example, Bentley cars only service up-market consumers so that price conscious consumers or value seekers are not served. This is evidenced through their marketing strategy and the types of product that are being offered to the marketplace.

Customized marketing is where the marketing mix is designed to appeal to individual customers. This type of marketing campaign is usually used in B2B markets, where the orders gained are contractual, often long-term, and usually of high value. For example, Siemens designs and configures electronic component parts to attract large car manufacturers but then markets their offer to each customer individually, based on the customer's needs, to provide a solution in line with their requirements.

Positioning

Positioning concerns the act of designing the organization's offering so that it occupies a distinct position within its customers'

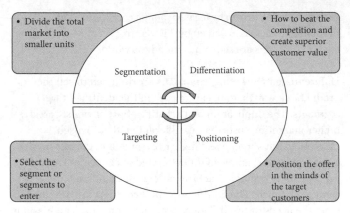

5. Positioning in relation to segmentation and targeting.

minds. Positioning is the way in which the customer perceives the organization's offer compared with competitive products and is the act of linking the organization's products and services to the solutions that the customer seeks (see Figure 5).

To successfully position the product in the customer's mind, marketers need to build a clear picture of the offer, its benefits and features. The positioning of the product emphasizes how this product is different from those of their competitors. For example, North Face clothing company positions itself at the fashionable, stylish end of the durable, wet weather clothing market, which is different from their competitors Rohan or Mountain Equipment. Once a position has been established it becomes a powerful marketing concept and the foundation for all related marketing and brand messages. A strong positioning statement will help to clarify the value of the product to the market, what that product is expected to deliver in terms of value compared to its competitors. The disadvantage of a strong positioning statement is that it is very difficult to change once it has become established. For example, British Airways wanted to change their image to something more fun and colourful, so they painted the tailfins of their aircraft with vibrant designs and changed their publicity statements. Unfortunately, their customers' reaction was universally negative as they felt that the 'Britishness' of the brand was being undermined.

Successful positioning will have four characteristics:

- Clarity: a distinct set of values that are related to that offer only.
- Consistency: the values are always evident throughout the customers' interactions with the business.
- Credibility: the positioning and values are believable.
- Competitiveness: the values are superior to your competitors in meeting the segment's needs.

A value proposition is a promise of the benefits to be delivered, communicated, and acquired from interacting with a specific product or brand, which is supported by the positioning statement. Developing a value proposition is based on the evaluation of the potential benefits of the offer against its associated costs (Value = Benefits − Costs). Michael Lanning and Edward Michaels, who worked for McKinsey, explained that the value proposition is a statement which conveys clear, measurable, and demonstrable benefits to the customer of the business's offer, which may also be communicated through the organization's brand (see Chapter 4). Therefore, the marketer links the offers to the solutions that the customers are seeking, and this would be supported by the brand of the organization or product group. For example, Intel's brand name conveys that the internal chip provided by Intel inside the computer will outperform its competitors and is therefore a desirable addition to the manufacturer's product.

What is branding?

Branding is associated with creating and communicating a three-dimensional character for a business, goods, or services that is not easily copied or damaged by competitors' efforts. A brand is not just a logo or name, it is everything that the organization does. It is also a promise and commitment to customers and therefore should be the whole organization's concern. The brand is a representation of the organization's culture as it is based on the values that are important to it. A brand helps a product or organization to stand out in the marketplace and creates a lasting impression in the minds of its customers in order to raise the organization's visibility. The objective of branding is to provide an indication of the experience and benefits that the customer should have while engaging with that organization's offers.

The aim of a brand is to create an identity and personality for the brand, which is supported by the marketing mix. Brand identity comprises the elements that make it easily identifiable such as the logo, colours, and slogans. Brand personality is its character, for example being warm, friendly, sociable, or innovative. One of the most effective brand marketing organizations in the world is Coca-Cola. There is little difference in the core product of cola. However, Coca-Cola is completely distinguishable through its brand's identity—the name, the colour red, distinctive lettering on the packaging and logo, the shape of the glass bottle—and the accompanying advertising of its personality (image) of celebration and its reflection of American values. The brand identity for the soft drink Irn-Bru is another good example. Its values are conveyed through highlighting its distinctive taste, its logo, and bright orange colour, as well as its Scottish personality and heritage, and the implications of conferred strength through 'Irn' (iron) in its name. Successful brands can aid product identification, create customer loyalty, and facilitate premium pricing, as well as helping to defend the organization's position against its competitors.

Each year information on the top global brands is published (see Table 4). This ranking confirms the contribution that creating

Table 4. Interbrand's top ten global brands by brand value (2019)

Rank	Brand	Value (US$ million)
1	Apple	234,240
2	Google	167,713
3	Amazon	125,263
4	Microsoft	108,847
5	Coca-Cola	63,365
6	Samsung	61,098
7	Toyota	56,246
8	Mercedes-Benz	50,832
9	McDonald's	45,362
10	Disney	44,352

and managing a top brand makes to organizational value. Brand recognition is about the consumer's ability to identify a particular brand and link it to the associated goods and services. If a consumer is aware of a brand, they are able to identify its category and distinguishing features to make an emotional connection with it.

A strong brand also provides the opportunity for brand extensions, where other product groups are added to the brand's portfolio. For example, Colgate was known for providing toothpaste but now they also manufacture mouthwash and toothbrushes using the same brand name. How far a brand should be extended is a matter for debate. Dyson has successfully extended their brand from vacuum cleaners to hand dryers, hair dryers, and portable fans. They are all in a similar manufacturing area—air management—so it seems to work, but what would happen if they produced Dyson clothing or Dyson bikes? Dyson would have to decide if the brand would be suitable for these product groups and, if they continue to use this brand name, will its value be diluted or not?

According to Philip Kotler, a brand's identity may deliver four different levels of meaning:

1. *Attributes*—these are the labels that the business wishes to be associated with, including the colour red and writing in a particular font for Coca-Cola.
2. *Benefits*—these are the emotional links created by the brand to the customer and consumer. In Coca-Cola's case a refreshing, fun drink.
3. *Values*—these are the core values of the brand or organization, such as efficiency, being trustworthy, supporting green issues, or taking an ethical stance. In Coca-Cola's case, it is being trustworthy and American.
4. *Personality*—these are what the brand would look like if it was a person, such as exciting, serious, hardworking, sophisticated, or innovative. In Coca-Cola's case, celebratory.

When used together these four aspects provide a powerful message to customers and competitors about what the organization or product stands for, and why it should be purchased in preference to other offers on the market. However, Philip Kotler also warned that once a strong brand has been established it needs constant attention and updating so that the brand values do not decay over time and remain relevant in the face of new and disruptive competition. For more information on branding, see *Branding: A Very Short Introduction*.

Chapter 4
Consumer and buyer behaviour and the value proposition

The importance of understanding both consumer and buyer behaviours is central to marketers creating effective marketing campaigns because the behaviours of consumers (end users of products) and B2B buyers (purchasers of products for business use) are different. Consumer and buyer behaviours are those actions undertaken when obtaining and consuming goods and services. By understanding how consumers think and how they behave during decision-making and purchasing activities, the marketer is able to exert some influence over their actions. Likewise, marketers can influence B2B purchasing patterns through their understanding of the behaviour of buyers.

Consumer decision-making process

Consumer behaviour is best understood through the following key elements: (1) identifying the consumer's motivation—their needs and wants; (2) decision-making—how they make choices; (3) post-purchase behaviours—what they do afterwards.

Most people make their purchasing decisions actively, as there are always some thought processes that precede the decision. The decision to make a purchase starts with the recognition that there is a need for some product to satisfy a deficiency. This is followed by a search for information on possible solutions and an

Problem Recognition	• I am hungry
Information Search	• What type of snacks are there here? Chocolate, Cereal bars or Cakes
Information Evaluation	• Based on my previous experiences do I want Chocolate, Cereal bars or a Cake?
Decision	• I will purchase a Cereal bar
Post Purchase Evaluation	• Was the Cereal bar good at satisfying my hunger and would I have one again?

6. The buying decision-making process.

evaluation of that information, which may also include taking influencers' opinions into account. A decision is then made, and the item purchased. The buying process is completed, but the consumer will then engage in a post-purchase evaluation of the product's performance to decide how satisfied they are with it, which will inform the next purchase in that area (see Figure 6).

The problem recognition part of the decision-making process links to the motivation to purchase in order to satisfy a need, want, or desire. The type of deficiency that needs to be addressed will influence whether the motivation is an urgent need or a less urgent want. For example, if you feel thirsty you will carry out an urgent search for something to drink to satisfy this need. An example of a want would be to go on holiday, while a desire may be to go to Australia. You may be able to fulfil a want to go on a holiday quite quickly with a little planning, but fulfilling your desire to go to Australia may take longer, as it is geographically further away and costly to get there, so you may need to take more time to save up to fund the trip, and to plan and prepare for it.

The process of searching for information will depend on the motivation and context. Buying decisions can be either low involvement (simple) or high involvement (complex). The level of involvement of the decision-making process is usually related to the value of the product being purchased and how critical it is to the buyer to make the correct choice. When searching for information, the purchaser goes through the same process, but if the purchase is a high involvement one the search is likely to take longer and be more wide-ranging. A low involvement purchase could be an impulse buy, like a chocolate bar, because you fancy a snack and with this type of purchase the search is likely to be very rapid. For a more high involvement, complex purchase such as selecting a holiday destination or buying a new car, the search is likely to take considerably more time, because the purchaser will want to collect more information on the choices available, make comparisons, and gather opinions from various influencers, before making the selection, as more is at risk and the investment is greater.

The next stage in the decision-making process will be to evaluate the alternatives and make a selection. For low involvement products, this is likely to be a quick evaluation of what is immediately available (which chocolate bars are on the shelf), perhaps with reference to previous experiences of eating these types of chocolate bar. For high involvement products the evaluation is likely to take longer, and involve collecting other people's recommendations and opinions, as well as reviewing relevant promotional literature for the best offers available. The selection in both cases will be the end of the evaluation stage and will be followed by the purchase. Again, the length of time that the selection and purchase takes will depend on the level of involvement in the product—with low involvement products, the buyer simply picks up the good and pays for it as appropriate. For high involvement products, the selection may be followed by a discussion of purchasing options with the seller, setting up a payment method, and negotiating the delivery of the goods or services.

The final part of the decision-making process is the post-purchase evaluation. For most purchases there is a review of the performance of the product. For our purchase of the chocolate bar this may consist of checking that it has satisfied your need for a snack and that it tasted good. This information will then influence your next purchase in similar circumstances. For high involvement products, the evaluation is likely to be lengthy once the process has been completed. The purchaser may also suffer from post-cognitive dissonance, which is the concern that they have made the wrong purchase. Depending on the value of the product, this post-purchase evaluation could even take years. Regularly, friends and family can highlight the benefits of the car that they have purchased, or express concerns about some of its flaws and features years after it was bought.

Consumer purchasing behaviour

Consumer behaviour is how the potential buyer approaches making a decision to purchase something for their own use. This process impacts on how goods and services are consumed or experienced by the purchaser. Philip Kotler explains that consumer buying decisions do not happen in isolation, they are conditioned by a number of influences. Culture will be a major influence on our decision-making, as this will guide what it is acceptable to purchase (see Figure 7).

Culture is made up of learned values, perceptions, needs, and behaviours of every member of a particular group. National cultures are quite clearly defined and provide different needs, wants, and demands in various geographical regions. National cultures also have subcultures with shared values that can further alter consumers' buying behaviours. A subculture is a group of people with shared value systems, or common life experiences, such as Goths, football fans, followers of heavy metal music, or even bikers, as they have specific characteristics that give them unique preferences for particular products. These subcultures can provide important market segments for the marketer to target, as the product can be designed around the preferences of subcultures

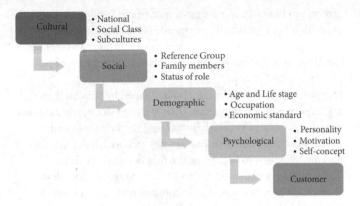

7. Influences on purchasing behaviours.

with the marketing messages adjusted to meet their needs, such as Harley-Davidson who successful target the subculture of older 'American culture' motorbike riders.

Culture and subcultures indicate which groups are most important in influencing purchasing trends, as well as individual decisions. In some cultures, employers have the most significant influence, while in others, society at large has the greatest sway on opinion, conveyed through governmental messages, social media, and the national press, such as the anti-drink-and-drive campaigns run by the UK government every Christmas. Beyond cultural and subcultural influences on what we buy, we are influenced by the people closest to us, such as our immediate family and friends, and by groups who are important to us, such as our reference group.

The reference group is considered to be the people or person that has the highest impact on our behaviours and provides the standards and norms against which we judge ourselves and adjust our attitudes. Most of us will wish to fit into a particular group or groups, and we often find that we are 'taken along with the crowd' on a number of decisions about how we live our lives. Reference groups can be small, consisting of immediate family members and close friends, or perhaps key associates from work or leisure activity groups. Some reference groups can be large and include social sets or class, internet communities, or religious groups.

Our purchasing decisions can also be shaped by opinion leaders and experts who are important to us and who frequently use mass media and social networks to communicate their views and preferences (see Figure 8). Rating sites such as TripAdvisor can also host discussions regarding the functions and quality of various offers, and consumers will often engage in 'chat' about their recent purchases, and post opinions and experiences. How much we 'listen' to all of these influences will depend on our psychological attitudes.

One of the most important influences on our decision-making is our perception of how we should act in different situations. Our perception is the process by which we select and interpret information so that we can make sense of the world. Consequently, perception is shaped by our personal life experience and education. Every day we make thousands of selection decisions as we are bombarded by new and repeated information and choose

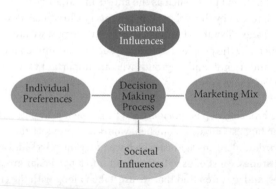

8. Influencers of buying decisions.

to pay attention to some aspects and ignore others. These selection decisions shape our perception of the world and how we can fit into it. It is this selection process that marketers hope to influence and benefit from, as by sending messages that will resonate with the target group of consumers (customer segment) they hope to fit with the consumers' perception of things that are important to them.

Our purchase decisions are also influenced by our immediate situation. An emergency situation, such as your car breaking down, will create an urgent need to make a complex decision rapidly. You may decide to purchase the nearest available vehicle that meets your basic criteria, without considering some other important factors such as the servicing options or prestige of the brand. Alternatively, purchases may be driven by special occasions, such as a religious festival, national holiday, or personal event, such as a birthday or anniversary, which will dictate when purchasing decisions have to be made. Consequently, marketing needs to understand how consumers buy, when they buy, where they buy, and what influences their buying habits.

The influence of marketing on consumer behaviour

The targeted marketing mix aims to guide the potential purchasers to consider certain products. Promotional efforts can entice purchasers to buy, but their personal experiences of previous purchases and their relationship with the brand may also condition how this is approached. Although most purchases are made in response to personal needs, they can be affected by the groups that we are members of, or those to which we aspire. This really illustrates that buying decisions are partially driven by rational (what do I need), behavioural (what have I done before), and emotional (what do I want) responses to offers. For example, we may buy black or green wellington boots to keep our feet dry but may buy boots in bright pink with white spots to represent our feelings and personality.

One way in which marketers can influence consumers is to individually target each part of the decision-making process. First, marketers will want to raise awareness of their products through branding, advertising, PR, and word of mouth recommendations from recognized influencers, so that they feature in the search part of the decision-making process. An example would be the continuous advertisements on television, radio, online, and in the press for insurance products. Marketers do not know when consumers will be looking for this type of product, as every year insurances are updated at the time that they were originally purchased. Consequently, marketers use continuous marketing to ensure that their name is in mind when the renewal comes around. During the search for information stage, marketers also want accurate information to be readily available on webpages, search engines, and for social media recommendations to be positive. For example, TripAdvisor reviews may affect our selection of hotels or restaurants. During evaluation, buyers may be influenced to make a selection by the brand's reputation, salespeople's expertise, flexible pricing options, and/or accessible distribution.

Selection may be influenced by discussions with family and friends, but marketers can still influence the final selection through enticing sales promotions (discounts, special offers, or gifts), as well as positive social media site endorsements and loyalty marketing. One of the biggest growth areas to influence consumer purchasing in recent years is the use of loyalty cards and reward programmes. Many organizations, especially in the hospitality, travel, and retail industries, use loyalty cards that confer a quasi-membership on the consumer that entitles them to preferential treatment, free gifts, or other forms of enticement. Its purpose is to encourage the repeated selection of the organization's offer over its competitors, which helps to retain consumers and make sure that they are loyal to a particular brand. The actual purchase is primarily influenced by efficient processes, distribution, and customer services. Finally, the post-purchase evaluation is conditioned by the product's performance, reassurance through confirmatory promotional messages, and efficient customer services. Consequently, the marketer can use different parts of the marketing mix to influence each part of the decision-making process.

Buyer behaviour, business-to-business

The buying decision-making process in B2B situations is affected by its context. Consumers are usually individuals who purchase to meet a personal need or want. An organizational buyer will usually purchase to meet a group or organizational need, and therefore the decision will often involve several interrelated parties, including initiators, influencers, buyers, decision-makers, and users (see Table 5). This means that buyers will have to negotiate with others within the organization as well as negotiating with the supplier. The use of a buying 'committee' or buying decision-making unit, especially for expensive or unique products, means that salespeople may find it difficult to find out what their business buyers want and how to influence them.

Table 5. Participators in the purchase of industrial products

Roles in the decision-making unit	Function
The initiator	The person who proposes that there is a need that can be filled by a particular purchase.
The influencer	People with expert opinion who provide guidance.
The decision-maker	The person with the authority to make the purchase.
The buyer	The person who places the order.
The user	The person who consumes the product.

The business market has a number of unique features that change the buying behaviours of participants. The most common B2B purchases are for production or for resale. The type of purchase that is made for production includes new machinery (capital goods), raw materials, and services such as IT systems. A purchase for resale is where a product is purchased at trade price and then resold at a higher price to another buyer or consumer. The value of the B2B market is large because for every consumer product purchased, there are many business purchases that support its production. Car manufacturers will have to purchase engine components, tyres, seat fabrics, steel and carbon fibre, glass, door mechanisms, drive trains, electrics and electronic brain, plastics and accessories to make one car.

The manufacturer will also need to purchase capital goods, such as production and operating machinery, and provide storage and transportation for the finished goods. All these goods and services have to be bought at the right price and quality. However, it is important to note that demand for these production products will depend on the consumers' demand for the final product (which is called derived demand).

The buying process in a B2B context is subject to several organizational 'checks and balances' to ensure that the best purchase at the best price is made for the business, and consequently the buying process is considered to be less emotionally driven than consumer purchasing. Organizations put a lot of procedures and practices in place to reduce the effects of human emotions in business purchasing behaviour. However, it has been found that emotions still play an important role in buying decisions. Tesco and Walmart, for example, rotate the personnel in their buying teams on a regular basis so that purchasing decisions are based purely on business needs and performance, rather than on their relationship with salespeople. The sales function is closely allied to the marketing function in B2B companies and many organizations have employed dedicated sales teams to manage their B2B relationships and interactions (see Chapter 5).

Another unique feature of the business market is that the products and their purchase are usually complex. Purchases frequently include a number of individual negotiations for a variety of component parts, and they are sometimes dependent on the supply of complementary or supplementary products. The complexity of the items to be purchased means that some suppliers are offering solution bundles. This is where the manufacturer purchases several components from one supplier, who will compile the necessary parts and put them together to sell on in a single offer, such as a computer supplier providing an organization with a computer network made up of components from different manufacturers. This practice makes the solution bundle valuable to the buyer, as its purchase saves them time negotiating with a range of different contractors. It benefits the supplier as well, as they can charge more for the whole solution or bundle than for individual elements.

According to Wim Biemans, a leading expert in B2B marketing, three factors dominate the buying behaviours in B2B markets: (a) buy class; (b) product type; and (c) the importance of the purchase to the purchaser. 'Buy class' can be a rebuy, new buy, or modified rebuy. If the purchase is a rebuy (repeated purchase), the buyer may be the only person involved in the purchase, because the supplier and product are well known so there is little need to negotiate and the paperwork is already in place. Conversely, a new buy might involve the full decision-making unit outlined in Table 5, as the specifications, terms, and prices will be open to negotiation and often to competition between suppliers. The buying process for a new buy will consequently take longer to negotiate and be more complex because there are more people's opinions to be taken into account before a decision is made. A modified rebuy falls somewhere between a rebuy and new buy, and is where the repeated purchase needs to be altered in some way in response to changing conditions or updates to the product.

The product type, its function, and whether it is a good or a service will condition the nature of purchase being made and its purchase frequency. The importance of the purchase to the organization will be determined by the value (benefits) the purchase confers, its overall cost, and relative scarcity. The higher the importance of the purchase to the organization the more time, people, and effort will be put into the decision-making process.

Creating a value proposition

As mentioned previously, marketing strategies need to be customer driven and focused on the nature of the value that is being proposed. Customer value is the satisfaction that the customer experiences when they make a purchase, relative to the cost of that purchase. A value proposition is a statement of the expected benefits for the customer (consumers and buyers) of purchasing a particular product, which can be used to successfully commercialize a product offer. The expected benefits can include attributes such as performing specific functions, including the level of quality anticipated, and the associated feelings generated by the purchase of a product, for example prestige, excitement, satisfaction, contentment, and trust.

The term 'value proposition' was first introduced by Lanning and Michaels, when they outlined that businesses are actually managed value delivery systems. The value proposition itself is the promise to deliver a set of benefits (both tangible and intangible) that the customer will appreciate and that will attract them to the offer. There are many advantages to having a clear value proposition, including the fact that it quickly communicates what you do, reassures your customers that they will be getting the best value for money, and conveys to them how this purchase will resolve a pain point for this potential customer (see Figure 9).

9. Mailchimp value proposition.

A value proposition is one way of conveying the offer's unique selling points to the market by outlining how this offer is different and/or superior to their competitors' offers. To provide information on what should be in the value proposition, the following questions should be considered:

1. What does the target group need from our product?
2. What are the benefits that the customer would appreciate?
3. What pains are they trying to avoid or what problems do they want to solve?
4. What are we going to produce to meet those needs?
5. How does this offer outperform our closest competitors?

To create a focused value proposition that is attractive and compelling to the target customers, marketers should consider three stages:

(i) Identify the exact benefits that the customer will enjoy.
(ii) Link those benefits to the mechanisms that will convey them to the customer.
(iii) Map the benefits that highlight the basis of their differentiation in the marketplace.

Philip Kotler suggests that to create a winning value proposition it is necessary to adjust the price and benefits offered in comparison to those of your competitors. The most advantageous positions would be to offer more benefits to customers at a higher price than competitors in order to generate the most profit. Alternatively, offering the same price or lower price than competitors with more or equal benefits will also work, but the individual profit margins are likely to be lower. Offering the same benefits at the same price as competitors will only add value if there is some kind of exclusivity, such as a specific brand or location advantage.

The value proposition statement should then be written explaining the relevance of the offer to solving the customers' problems, the quantifiable benefits (value), and how these differ from your competitors' offers. One suggestion is that there should be a headline title that is eye-catching and covers what is being offered and to whom in one short sentence. The headline title should be followed by a two- to three-sentence paragraph explaining what is being offered, who can benefit, and why this solves a problem/meets a need. The next part of the value proposition could include bullet points or a diagram that clearly outlines and quantifies the key benefits. Somewhere in the presentation there should be an attention-grabbing visual such as an image of the product or its application (see Figure 9).

The value proposition should be shown at every entry point into your organization, on the website, in direct mail (emails, text messages, or letters), catalogues, on point of sale promotions, and in advertising. In fact, the value proposition should appear anywhere that the target group is likely to engage with the organization. However, the value proposition is not a mission statement or brand slogan, as it is only aimed at the target customers and conveys why they should buy from you and not your competitors. The Australian academics, Adrian Payne and Penny Frow, explained that another function of the value proposition is to ensure that the whole organization understands what the organization is selling, so they are able to contribute to the creation of that value. In the Mailchimp example this would be an all-in-one marketing platform to help small businesses grow through creating and managing mailing lists, newsletters, and automated marketing campaigns. The key is that it helps the organization to understand what has to be achieved and the customer to understand what is being offered, fostering transparency in their relationship.

The theory is that value is created for both the customer and the supplier, and they should both benefit from the transaction, financially and intrinsically. It is possible to measure if the value of the proposition is positive or negative by calculating the financial worth of the benefits less the associated costs of producing those benefits. To understand how the value proposition is understood in different business contexts (industries) there is a need for a systematic approach to developing propositions that are meaningful to the target segment. Going for an 'all-benefits' approach (communicating that everything that we do is superior to our competition) may be less effective than creating a value proposition that communicates the specific benefits that resonate with the target customer's explicit needs.

The value proposition must therefore be created with specific customers in mind and needs to be supported by marketing research. It should be used to identify the key functions of the offer, the benefits provided, and customer pain points to be serviced. The value proposition will not just differ from business unit to business unit, but also from product group to product group, and customer segment to customer segment. Each value proposition should be reviewed and updated regularly in a similar manner to brand values, as customers' needs do not remain static and competitors do not stand still. Customers will expect different benefits over time, as markets mature, customers' experiences alter, and competitors change their value propositions.

In the airline industry, customers of premier carriers such as BA, Lufthansa, and Cathay Pacific are offered the intangible values of being transported at a promised level of comfort, with attentive service and efficiency, and this value proposition is enhanced through gifts of physical products such as face masks, ear plugs, socks, toothpaste/brush, and additional food options. The budget airline carriers such as Ryanair, easyJet, and Southwestern have value propositions that emphasize their low cost and efficiency, with all other benefits available to be purchased. Value propositions provide the key to each organization's success by telling their customers the number one reason why they should select that product over the competition's, and indicating to both employees and customers what makes that organization or brand unique.

Chapter 5

Promotions (marketing communications) and social media

In the modern environment we are bombarded with around a million promotional messages every year that are designed to influence our behaviour. The aim of marketing communications (commonly known as Promotions in the four Ps) is to inform customers about the organization's latest products and offers, and other activities. We will also consider how promotions are used to convey the organization's brand messages internally and externally.

Promotions are made up of a range of communication tools which are critical in supporting the organization's offer and conveying their brand values. They are designed to reach, interest, and engage customers in conversations, and to encourage them to purchase products. Promotional tools include advertising, sales promotions, public relations, direct marketing (on- or offline), sponsorship, and personal selling. Each of these tools has different attributes, for example, sales promotions are the special offers that are made at the point of purchase and are often associated with encouraging impulse purchases. Conversely, PR is about conveying information regarding the values and activities of the organization by engaging with different media (newspapers, news agencies, and TV companies, as well as social media) in order to generate free publicity.

Communication activities are being totally reinvented by the growth of social media and digital marketing. Traditionally communication was one-way, from the seller to the buyer. However new technology has changed all that, and digital marketing enables two-way interaction between the organization and the customer. Social media is the integration of technology to create something of value and can be comprised of company and consumer generated content conveyed by a platform, for example YouTube, Facebook, Twitter, Instagram, and the company's website. Inviting audiences to post comments on events, post videos, and upload photographs and live tweets enables people to engage with the organization. The development of different types of social media has created opportunities to develop digital marketing that has an immediacy of interaction and increased intimacy with potential customers. In today's world social media has gained enormous importance and influence, and the lines between real life and virtual reality are becoming more blurred every day.

What are promotions?

Promotions are probably the marketer's most visible activity. Promotions or marketing communications come totally within the responsibility of the marketing department and are seen to be more controllable than the other elements of the marketing mix. They are used to communicate with the organization's stakeholders, both internally and externally. The promotional mix is made up of the various communication tools (see Figure 10).

The promotional campaign is a sequence of activities that reflects a common theme, so that the right messages are conveyed to the target group effectively. For example, a travel company may use TV advertising, social media, and e-marketing to connect with a group of younger customers interested in adventure holidays;

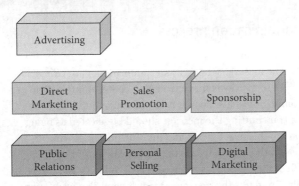

10. Key promotional mix tools.

while selecting TV and radio advertising, brochures, and direct mail to reach an older target group interested in cruises.

Setting objectives for promotional campaigns is a key role of the marketer, as it requires a clear understanding of what the organization needs to achieve and how the promotional mix can encourage potential customers to purchase. Different objectives may include building product or brand awareness, countering competitors' offerings, and initiating a trial or retrial of new offers. Overall, promotional campaigns will aim to make their organization the supplier of choice for potential customers and, in this way, the organization can increase its market share (the market share is the proportion of the total potential market that purchase the organization's offer rather than the competitors' offers). Promotional campaigns, through tools such as social media and sales promotions, stimulate immediate sales or create sustained product preference. Of course, the consistency of the promotional mix will rely on the resources available to the organization and the cost of obtaining these, as well as the customer's informational needs, the market size, and the product/brand characteristics. All these elements will guide the marketer to select the most appropriate promotional tools to meet the target group's needs.

The communication process

The communication process is a key concept for promotions (see Figure 11). The message (thought, idea, information, or concept) that you want to convey is first encoded or changed into a form (words, sound, or visuals) so that it can be transmitted. The method of transmitting the message should be selected as being appropriate to the target group and may include employing newspapers, radio, email, television, billboards, and/or social media. When the message is received it is decoded by the receiver, and ideally it remains the message that was sent. The problem is that the message received is not always the same as the one that the sender intended to convey, due to distortion during transmission or misunderstandings by the receiver, which affects the meaning of the marketing message.

As a result, it is important to generate feedback that will clarify whether or not the correct message has been received. All messages are received against a background of 'noise'. Advertising noise is created by all the different advertising messages being sent by competitors, other institutions, and individuals. There may also be other types of noise interference created through

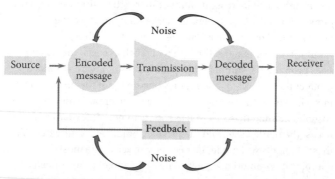

11. The communication process.

physical or psychological barriers, such as poor image quality or a distracted receiver. As a result, marketers aim to design messages so that they are appropriate for the receiver and cut through the surrounding 'noise'. Marketers will often pre-test and post-test any promotional campaign to find out if the messages that they intended to communicate have been received by customers and correctly understood.

Advertising

Advertising is paid-for media that is used to convey messages that interest target customers, raise awareness of the organization/product, communicate information, and generate sales. Advertising is used to convey open (non-personal), paid-for messages to mass target audiences through a range of media, including newspapers, television, radio, external advertising hoardings, and the internet, including blogs, social media sites, websites, and pop-ups. Any messages sent through these purchased media should be consistent with the brand values and provide a focused communication that encourages the purchase of, or engagement with, the organization's offer. Because of the range of different media available to convey adverts it is possible for the marketer to select those that will be most effective in reaching their target group(s). For example, advertisers of holiday cottages are likely to target magazines such as *Country Living* and holiday web searches, while multivitamins and sports equipment are more likely to be advertised on television and in health magazines.

Adverts should be configured so that they are attractive and stand out from all the advertising 'noise' in the market. 'Share of voice' is where marketers try to match or exceed each other's advertising spend in order to have the loudest voice. Adverts have become more and more outrageous, exciting, or sophisticated in order to stand out from the crowd, and they employ different combinations of sound, colour, images, words, and movement.

12. Cadbury Gorilla advert.

One of the most effective advertising campaigns was run by Cadbury Chocolates in 2000 (see Figure 12). The advertisement used a visual of a gorilla playing a set of drums to a Phil Collins hit track. This was a risky strategy as there was no obvious link between the musical gorilla and a chocolate bar. However, this advert transformed the future of the Cadbury organization. The advert made people feel very happy, and there was a subliminal message that chocolate will release those same sorts of happy feelings. This advert stood out because of the music and lyrics, and its apparent randomness, but there were still strong links to the product through the use of the brand's signature purple colour in the background and the final image of a chocolate bar.

Total advertising spend in 2019 was around $560 billion, a small increase on the previous year. According to Global Advertising Spend 2010–18, the largest contributor to global advertising spend is the US, followed by China (about half that of the US), then Japan, the UK, and Germany. As advertising is so successful in bringing products and issues to the attention of potential customers, and advertising has become so efficient and prolific, we have become very good at screening out (ignoring) messages that are not particularly interesting to us. This is termed consumer apathy or selective attention. To overcome consumer apathy, organizations may utilize different psychological techniques, such as promoting exclusivity or fear, for example, by creating special flavours for crisps that are only available for a short time, introducing uncertainty, and running emotional ideas such as selling dreams/fantasies rather than reality.

One form of advertising that may be a little less obvious is the role of product placement. This is where branded products are placed in films, videos, and TV productions so that they become associated with that production or its celebrities. Product placement may be explicit, such as in the James Bond films which often include extensive footage of Aston Martin cars. Alternatively, placements may be more subtle, for example a sign or logo being shown in the background of a key shot, the distinctive Coca-Cola bottle being placed on a table, or the key character wearing a particular brand of clothing. Of course, product placements must be handled carefully by the marketers, or the production may become overloaded with too many advertising messages so that none stands out.

Marketers use both rational (central) and emotional (peripheral) appeals to attract attention to their offer. The central method is the more rational/logical route that is mainly used to interest potential consumers in 'high-involvement', more costly products that will need considerable thought and evaluation before the purchase is made—for example, the purchase of a new vehicle, a major piece of equipment, property or furnishings, or a consultancy or legal services. Because the purchasing price is high the marketing messages are likely to be more informative, providing facts, figures, and reassurance about the quality of the offer.

Conversely, the peripheral route is more emotional and is more usually employed to attract consumers to 'low-involvement' products that are purchased frequently and at a lower relative cost. The marketing messages for these types of product may employ storytelling, colourful imagery, and exciting music, for example the John Lewis or Marks & Spencer Christmas adverts that have recurring themes of fun and happiness during the holiday period.

To reinforce their advertising messages (either low or high involvement), marketers are increasingly involving both opinion leaders and opinion formers to help to influence consumers' perceptions via social media. There are many advertisements that also depict opinion leaders (celebrities and specialists) using a particular offer or being employed to directly promote their offer. A sports athlete might promote a brand of relevant equipment or an expert might explain the benefits of a new product, for example dentists recommending particular toothpastes.

Sales promotions

Sales promotions are a useful tool to create a short-term boost in sales. Sales promotions are not a single tool, but a set of techniques to interest potential purchasers in a specific offer, which may include things such as discounts (everyone loves the two for one offer, which is commonly known as BOGOF or buy one, get one free), gifts, collectables, competitions with prizes and vouchers (or loyalty points), and free samples (see Figure 13). These offers can be aimed at consumers who are purchasing the offer for their own use, or at customers who buy the offer for resale. These are called trade promotions and are designed to increase the adoption of their offer by manufacturers.

Sales promotions are designed to increase impulse buying and can be successful in raising awareness and increasing sales for the term of the promotion. However, sales promotions should not be used too frequently, or the extra benefit provided by the offer will

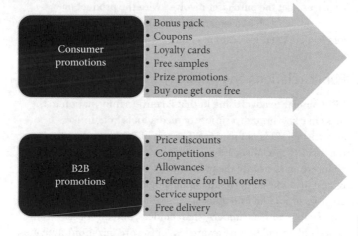

13. Consumer and B2B promotions.

quickly become established as the norm and expected by customers to be available at all times.

Sales promotions should be very carefully planned and executed. There is the infamous example of Hoover UK wishing to move extra units of their vacuum cleaners, and later washing machines, in the early 1990s. To do this they ran a promotional campaign offering free airline tickets with the purchase of these items. Unfortunately, the offer was so well received, mainly because the airline tickets cost about the same or more than the items on offer for sale, that the organization oversold the promotion. Consequently, they made a huge financial loss on the promotion and totally lost control of its delivery, leaving them with lawsuits for breach of contract as well as very bad publicity.

Free samples or loss leaders may be employed effectively, particularly around the launch of a new product. Free samples are popular for products in the lower price brackets, such as cosmetic products attached to magazines. Loss leaders may be employed as a teaser to get the purchaser involved with the product or organization, such as a supermarket running milk and bread as loss leaders to entice customers into their store.

Public relations and publicity

PR is similar to advertising in that it conveys information to the mass market through a variety of media tools but, unlike advertising, PR is not paid for. The aim of PR, according to one of the first PR specialists, Edward Bernays, is to spread information by inserting ideas into the public's consciousness through releasing stories to the media in the hope that they will be passed on or incorporated into other news stories. PR is used to build connections with customers, shareholders, and any other stakeholders and to raise awareness of the organization's activities. A good example of PR would be an organization promoting a new product launch (such as a new car model) and inviting journalists and news writers to attend and sample the offer. The expectation would be that a review of the new product would be provided in the media over the subsequent few days by the journalists who attended the launch.

The work of the public relations specialist is to create and maintain positive relationships with key media specialists, to keep track of opinion leaders and relevant trade media events in their field, and to advise the executives of the organization how to handle any dealings with the media. The role may include writing press releases, designing communication campaigns, arranging interviews, writing speeches, managing social media content, managing the organization's reputation (including crises management), and handling the publicity for media events (such as sponsorship events). PR is usually the tool that is used when the organization needs to respond to a crisis or has to convey bad news, such as the KFC 'We are Sorry' campaign which was run when KFC's supply chain let them down in 2018. Further, governments frequently use PR to convey messages of public interest, such as information on the HIV virus, or to try to influence public opinion.

To undertake PR activities, marketers will need to understand the concerns and interests of the organization's stakeholders and how they relate to the organization's brand, aims, and objectives. PR has traditionally relied on media such as TV, radio, and press journals and newspapers, but now they also have to be versed in the use of social media and other digital media. Although the effectiveness of PR is difficult to gauge numerically, the Public Relations Society of America suggested that it is possible to measure engagement through feedback (such as 'likes', and 'social comments'), impressions (how widely spread knowledge of the item is), reach (how a news piece spreads through various media), mentions (number of appearances of a news item in various media), and items (measuring any content, blogs, posts, etc.) that originated from digital media.

Sponsorship

This is another communications tool designed to attract attention by financially supporting an event, activity, person, or group that is in the public's eye. In return for financial support there is usually an opportunity to promote the organization in some way, perhaps by displaying their logo or by mentioning their products. Some sponsored events may be allied to the organization's business or industry, but others may simply offer the opportunity for public exposure to help increase customer awareness of the organization or to build brand. It is important in sponsorship deals that both parties understand what is involved, what is required, and what the possible outcomes might be. There are also some challenges to undertaking sponsorship agreements. If the group/individual being sponsored fails to deliver the expected success or is associated with a scandal, then the sponsor may become associated with their failure and possibly gain negative publicity. Additionally, it is notoriously difficult to measure the effectiveness of sponsorship in raising awareness of the brand or product in the minds of potential customers. For example, when Tiger Woods was experiencing marital problems and his behaviour was reported in the press, General Motors and AT&T ended their sponsorship deals with him.

One of the benefits of sponsorship is that the activity, for example a sports event or charity gala, can make the potential customer feel positive, and these good feelings are then linked to the organization's name. In theory, the larger the amount of financial support that the sponsor provides, the greater the coverage the organization receives at the event. The main sponsor of an international event, such as the Olympics, may negotiate the right to use the image of the event in their own promotions, for example 'Coca-Cola, official sponsor of the Olympics'. In 2016, Panasonic paid $350 million for an eight-year, four-Olympic Games sponsorship deal (summer and winter).

Direct marketing

Direct marketing provides the opportunity for the marketer to communicate directly with their customers and consumers. Direct marketing may take place in a number of ways, for example online, flyers, postal mail, and text messages. The big advantage of direct marketing is that the response to the promotion can be measured, especially when it requires the customer to return a voucher, provide a comment, or apply for an offer. The other advantage of direct marketing is that it is possible to target the relevant customer segment very closely and present them with a clear value proposition. The growth of the internet has made direct marketing cheaper and easier to manage (in terms of collating data on the respondents and measuring response rates), as every visitor to a website landing page can be measured and their subsequent actions tracked. Of course, the best response to a direct marketing campaign is to measure actual sales that result from the contact.

There are some issues involved with running direct marketing campaigns as customers become dissatisfied with the amount of contact that they are receiving (e.g. too many computer-generated e-messages such as spam, letters, and junk mail), or if the direct marketing message is not closely connected to the target group. The result is that the conversion rate from contact to sales is extremely poor. However, marketers continue to use direct marketing and recognize that there are financial benefits to increasing targeted awareness of the organization's offers.

Events marketing and exhibitions

This is where an organization will present its offers directly to consumers and customers at an interactive event. Participatory events allow direct contact between the organization and its buyers that relationships can be established and reinforced, questions answered, and new products shown and experienced. According to the Event Marketing Institute the largest type of marketing consumer events take place in national conference centres and will be designed to attract specific target customers, for example the Motor shows, Ideal Home exhibition, or CeBit. These large-scale events are widely publicized and attract thousands of potential purchasers over a two- to five-day period. The events are highly competitive as new products are presented to interested purchasers, and the exhibitors all try to have more attractive and exciting displays than their competitors.

In addition to these large-scale events there are smaller-scale, industry-based trade shows and exhibitions which are aimed directly at specific B2B customers. Trade fairs allow buyers to compare offers and strike new deals with their suppliers. Any type of marketing event or exhibition is very intensive and takes a considerable amount of time, staff, and resources to set up, but the majority of attendees indicate that they are more likely to buy the products being promoted at these events.

Personal selling

Personal selling occurs when a salesperson meets with a potential client/customer with the intention of engaging in a sales transaction/exchange. Unlike other traditional promotional activities, personal selling provides two-way communications with customers, which allows the salesperson to configure the sales pitch to meet the customer's requirements, as well as gathering market information and providing additional detail about the products being sold. The salesperson is a specialist member of the marketing team with skills in negotiation, relationship building, and interpersonal communications, as well as having considerable knowledge of the products and services offered by the organization. Sales transactions can be undertaken over the telephone and the internet, as well as via face-to-face interactions. Salespeople can be found in a number of contexts, including the place of business of the customer, at exhibitions, in retail premises, on the internet, or in the office. Wherever sales interactions take place, personal selling remains the most persuasive method available to the marketer for generating sales.

Digital marketing and social media

A large proportion of all advertising and marketing activities are now focused on online activities, due to digital marketing yields being high. Some of the benefits include the opportunity to 'click through' to the organization's website from other sites via paid advertising or search engines. There are a range of techniques to advertise online, including banners, pop-up adverts, video clips, and special offer emails, all of which frequently contain links to the organization's website. By responding to digital marketing, customers are opting to engage directly with the organization. Interactions with the organization's website also provide the opportunity to develop marketing research. Organizations are able to gather their own first party data about their customers' preferences, which may be used to provide customer profiles, behavioural analysis, and identify profitable target segments, as well as to help them measure how well they are doing in the market. Additionally, many media sites such as Google Analytics are able to provide metrics and data about the activities of digital participants.

The advantages of digital marketing are that it has a large reach and is instantaneous, and additions and changes can be continuously made. Marketing can identify topics relevant to target customers and focus communications around that topic. The top five world media sites for advertising are Google, Facebook, Alibaba, Amazon, and Tencent. According to a 2018 analysis, 40 per cent of client budgets are now used for online marketing, with a 20–30 per cent growth in digital content, while standard advertising spend is only growing by around 2 per cent per annum. An inherent problem with all online content is that there is a very small window in which to attract people's attention before they click away. For example, it is possible to provide advertisements in front of video clips via YouTube, but due to the option to reject an advertisement online, companies need their name and the purpose of the advertisement to be included in the first 3–5 seconds of its run.

Organizations look for a range of outcomes from digital marketing, which include:

- Gather prospective customers
- Engage current customers and prospects
- Raise your visibility as an expert
- Draw the attention of media and influencers
- Get people to sign up for your newsletter, seminars, events, or downloads (webinars).
- Demonstrate your influence by growing the number of people who like and follow your pages.

The relative advantages of both digital and traditional marketing are easy to identify. Both have a wide-scale, global reach to different groups of customers. However, traditional media may be more targeted to a particular user group or product and is centralized in its production. As a result, when the communication reaches the customer it could be out of date, as there is a time lag between the generation and distribution of content. In contrast, digital content offers a faster response rate and can be more quickly adapted to changing market needs.

Social media may be used as part of promotions and is where organizations can engage with their customers, and customers can provide feedback and respond to comments, which means that social media promotions are primarily comprised of customer content. For example, customer forums can be used to influence thinking or to provide a 'sounding board' for companies advertising on the web. Also, many organizations make use of social media to disseminate positive comments designed to influence individuals who use and review their products online, which can lead to the formation of loyal customer groups. Marketers can also track the engagement of potential customers with certain topics via their social media usage. Organizations often use cookies on websites to record customers' likes, follows, and interests to identify what they are looking for and provide advertisements and comments that are linked to their preferences, so that they can match this with what they are offering and meet the customers' needs.

One of the dangers of using social media as a tool is that marketers have less control over it than traditional media, where the content and distribution are usually controlled by the organization. There are issues with how some of the content on social media is generated. For example, Facebook has recently employed around 30,000 people to monitor content on its site and remove offending items. If any topic on social media goes viral, it is passed from person to person, social media site to social media site, until it is accessible around the world. The opportunities to create interpersonal links across continents are presenting businesses with affordable options that enable them to increase their credibility, spread their brand messages, and influence the perceptions of their customers. Therefore, in today's environment, businesses and brands will find it hard to compete without making use of digital marketing and social media.

Chapter 6
Price and place (managing channels)

The elements of price and distribution are important parts of marketing strategy, but they are frequently ignored or sidelined when marketing strategy is being formulated. Pricing is critical in that it directly relates to the revenues generated by the organization and consequently affects its profitability. Another feature of the price part of the marketing mix is that it frequently impacts or interrelates with the other parts of the mix. If the price is placed higher than the market average, it could imply that the product quality is superior to other offers on the market, and the product's features and benefits should reflect this. Further, a high price would mean that the distribution channels (retailers) are expected to be of high quality and the promotional marketing messages should also reflect the overall premium position of the offer and support the values of the brand. Price also has a strategic impact as it can be used to create competitive advantage in the marketplace by either undercutting the competition or supporting premium positioning statements. For example, while you can buy a Casio wristwatch, which is an effective timepiece, for £22.99, some customers are prepared to pay upwards of £6,000 for a Rolex wristwatch, because it is perceived to be of high quality and a status symbol.

Place decisions are about how the product reaches the customers and are therefore about forms of distribution. Distribution can be achieved through direct or indirect channels to market. A direct channel is straight from the producer to the consumer, while an indirect channel would be through a number of intermediaries such as wholesalers, retailers, and via the internet. Place can also be about the physical location where the customer can obtain goods and services, and this now includes websites. The key to selecting the right place is that the product is available where and when the customer expects to find it so that the product is easily accessible. The strategic choice for marketers is to select the place that is aligned with the values of the offer/brand and which adds value to the customer's interaction with the product, such as Apple stores that provide an interactive experience as well as somewhere to purchase their products.

Pricing

Pricing is central to the success of a marketing strategy as the pricing strategy selected will determine the level of sales and profit made by a specific product, or product group. However, the pricing strategy adopted by the marketing team will have to conform to the overall pricing conditions set by balancing the costs of production against the return expected by the organization. There is a basic equation that underpins this pricing decision:

Costs of production per unit + Required return (profit margin) = Base price

This is called a cost-plus approach and ensures that the supplier does not make a loss on the sale of that product. However, this type of pricing ignores the demand sensitivity of the marketplace and could result in a price that is too high for the market or ignores some customers' willingness to pay a higher price. It should be noted that pricing is also a dynamic part of the marketing mix, as it can easily be altered in response to fast-changing environments. Customers have been seeking more value from their purchases in recent years (receiving more for less). This is placing suppliers and retailers under a great deal of pressure to constantly reduce prices at the till (or on the internet). Unfortunately, although price cutting can increase sales volume, it can also reduce profits and sometimes lead to price wars with competitors. With the increasing competition from internet sellers undercutting retail prices, more and more producers need to find pricing strategies that will preserve their market position and their profits.

Working from the base price, marketers will select the price point that is going to position their offer in the marketplace against the competition, meet the expectations of customers and consumers, and provide the greatest potential return. The pricing strategy selected should meet a number of clear conditions. What are the financial goals of the company?

1. A 'for-profit' organization, such as those producing consumer goods, expects to create profits for shareholders by selling their products for a sum that is greater than the cost of production.
2. A 'not-for-profit' organization such as those carrying out research or providing education, only intends to cover its costs.
3. A 'charity' expects to raise the maximum amount of revenue for all their activities, which should be either carried out at the lowest possible cost or ideally generate no cost to be undertaken.

A second consideration when setting the price is that the selected pricing strategy should fit with the marketplace realities. The prices charged should match what the customer is willing to pay and be competitive with other offers on the market. However, sometimes providing the required features will generate high manufacturing costs, resulting in a final price that can be higher than many customers are willing to pay. For example, coffee machines that provide high quality, fresh-tasting coffee in various forms (cappuccino, Americano, latte, and mocha) are quite complex and costly to manufacture. Consequently, the final selling price of the machine is relatively high, which makes them less attractive to purchasers. To solve this problem, manufacturers will often sell these machines at a very small profit or even at the cost of production price, but will then sell the accompanying consumable items, such as coffee pods, with a generous mark-up to generate ongoing profits.

Pricing strategies

The pricing strategy does not necessarily provide a specific price point for the product, but is a general guide or price range. Benson Shapiro and Barbara Jackson suggested that marketers can adopt three different types of pricing mechanism to set the price, depending on the market situation and objective to be achieved. For example, *cost-based pricing* is where the price is low, maybe only just above cost of production, and marketers will promote the offer based on the low prices charged. The aim would be to gain the maximum amount of sales and a high market share at that price point.

Alternatively, marketers could use *competition-based pricing* where the price is set in comparison to the offers from their most powerful competitors. The organization would compare its product's features and benefits and set the price to position the product in the marketplace. The marketer would promote the value of the offer, aiming to differentiate their brand from their competitors and support the price point chosen. The third option is to adopt *market-based pricing*, which is where the price is aligned with what the customer expects to pay and the value that they are likely to gain from the product. The price should support the features and benefits of the offer in order to meet their customers' needs, wants, and demands. Within these three basic pricing mechanisms there are variations that may be employed under different circumstances, such as price skimming, follow my leader pricing, price leadership, or penetration pricing (see Table 6).

Table 6. Pricing strategies

Pricing strategies	Description	When appropriate
Premium-based pricing	The price charged is near the high end of the possible pricing for that product type.	It is used to enhance or reinforce the product's luxury image. The product is designer, extremely high quality, and/or exclusive.
Price leadership	You set the price in the market as you are the dominant player.	It is used when there is a dominant player (has the greatest market share) to set the price points for all offers.
Follow my leader pricing	The pricing is set to equal that of the most dominant player in the market and follows price changes.	When you are the second/third player in the market and competing on differentiation not price.
Predatory pricing	Charging very low (near cost) prices to undercut competitors' prices.	When the market is under threat from new competitors or to maintain market leadership.
Market- (or competitor-) based pricing	Evaluating the prices of similar products on the market to determine the price to be charged.	Use it to compare features and benefits of your offer in comparison to other offers to set the price higher or lower than competitors.
Differential pricing	Charging different prices to different customer groups depending on their ability/willingness to pay.	When the offer is consumed in different ways and when there is a shortage in certain sectors.

Complementary pricing	Where the price of one product is dependent or linked to a complementary product such as razors and razor blades or vacuum cleaners and vacuum bags.	The main product is sold at a lower than normal price/profit margin and the complementary products are sold at a higher profit margin to recoup any loss made on the main product.
Dynamic pricing	The price changes with demand and changes whenever required, even hourly.	When demand is high or supply limited the price rises, and vice versa.
Temporary pricing strategies		
Price skimming	The product is new to the market and innovative.	Charge a relatively high price to recoup the development costs early in the product lifecycle.
Penetration pricing	The price is set lower than the average for that product group to attract customers and then raised to market norm.	When launching a new product to gain market share or may be used to deter new competitors from entering the market.
Promotional pricing	Temporary change in prices to attract new customers.	Used when there is a downturn in sales to sell stock, or if competitors are gaining market share.

Chanel perfume and Breitling watches employ premium pricing strategies (market-based pricing), as both these brands and their products are of very high quality and value. Premium pricing is where very high prices are charged, with larger mark-ups (difference between the cost of production and sale price) that are in line with their brand values. However, they only expect to sell a relatively small quantity of the products as there is a limited market for products in their price bracket. An example of competition-based pricing can be observed in the consumer fuel market. Many of the larger retailers such as Tesco and Sainsburys sell fuel on their sites, but have set their prices slightly lower in comparison to the major fuel providers, such as Shell and BP.

Organizations like Lidl, Primark, and Megabus (see Figure 14) on the other hand are all examples of organizations that have adopted a low-cost pricing strategy, where profits on individual products are smaller, but the volume of their sales is much higher. However, companies need to be careful when advertising their offers. The advertisement from Megabus shown in Figure 14 was banned by the Advertising Standards Authority (ASA) in the UK when it was shown that as few as only one seat on some routes was actually available at the £1 price point. Megabus have now adjusted their advertisements in line with the ASA ruling.

An example of differential pricing can be taken from the travel industry, where for example train tickets can be priced much higher during peak travel times when business users most frequently travel, but the same journey may be actually sold at a lower price during the middle of the day. As seats on trains are limited at peak times, differential pricing encourages travellers to choose another time to travel. This attracts a different set of customers through lower price tickets—to use the service during quiet periods, as the trains still have to run during the day.

A more recent trend is the use of dynamic pricing. In the past, most prices were fixed, and one price was set that applied to all

14. Megabus advertising.

customers. The advent of internet selling and multiple ways of obtaining the product have resulted in prices that can be continually adjusted to meet the selling situation and market conditions. Hotels use dynamic pricing to sell rooms through brokers and internet sites, and they continually adjust prices depending on demand for rooms.

Another pricing technique is bundling, where several goods and services are put together into a single package for an all-inclusive, reduced price. Within the bundle some products will be sold at a discount, while others will be more profitable. This technique can increase profits because multiple items are sold, and slow-moving products can be sold more quickly with the more popular items. Examples may include mobile phone bundles sold with various service packages, or large ticket items such as vacuum cleaners being sold with companion products like a handheld unit or additional attachments.

Pricing mistakes

Experience has highlighted a number of marketing pricing mistakes that have had serious repercussions for the whole organization. One of the most common is weak control over promotional pricing strategies. Situations where promotions have been continued for too long, or where there are multiple discounting offers, have eroded the value of the product offer in the minds of their customers. An example may be furniture retailers that always appear to have sales or special offers on their products. Customers become unsure of what the correct price should be and will not purchase unless they think that they are getting a special deal. Another pricing mistake to avoid is to set or change prices based on poor market information. If the price is inconsistent with the expectations of the customer, it is unlikely to attract sales. A further danger is that the pricing strategy selected is not appropriate for the market situation, so that price increases are introduced at a time when the market is very price-sensitive, or the penetration price creates a price war with a competitor.

Temporary pricing strategies

Temporary pricing strategies are designed for use when a product is being launched or repositioned in the market. Skimming is used when the price of individual products is set to be highly profitable. The strategy may be used to recoup the cost of developing a new product when the organization has a unique offer and attracts early adopters with high disposable incomes who understand the value of the new offer. This can either be achieved rapidly or slowly, depending on how fast the adoption of the product is likely to be and how quickly the product is likely to be copied by competitors. When Dyson first launched its 'cyclone-based' vacuum cleaners, the prices were extremely high in comparison to existing vacuums on the market, but as the new technology proved to be successful, the price lowered as competitors entered the market with their own versions.

Penetration pricing works differently. The product is launched at an initially low price to attract customers in large numbers from competitors, with the intention of increasing prices to market levels once the product has created a demand and an established market share. When the new *OK* magazine was launched it was at a price that undercut the existing *Hello* magazine for several months, until *OK* was established in the market. They are now similarly priced (at around £2.20–£2.30). Again, penetration pricing can be undertaken either rapidly or more slowly, depending on the product and market conditions.

Promotional pricing is where the price of a product or set of products is temporarily changed to increase sales. Techniques include pricing for combination or multiple orders (e.g. BOGOF), bulk order discounts, percentage reductions, sales, and loss leaders (see Chapter 5). An organization can use a variety of pricing strategies to sell their products. From a marketing point of view, the objective is to have a price that reflects the standing of your product in the marketplace, or that reflects the customer's perception of the brand. The pricing strategy can also be selected to defend an existing market or to increase market share.

Place or distribution channels

Place decisions are about how the product is distributed to customers. Distribution involves the planning, implementation, and control of the flow of goods and services from the point of origin to the point of consumption. The aim of 'Place' is to find the most suitable channel for a specified product to reach the target customers and this must be achieved in a way that meets the needs of the customer and delivers a profit. Distribution of products is an essential part of the marketing mix and the product can be delivered directly, from the producer to the customer, or indirectly through intermediaries such as retail outlets, wholesalers, or internet channels. Place decisions include the choice of retail location, position of the product within the store or catalogue/websites. It is important that the product is placed in a display that feels right, so care needs to be taken to avoid it being located alongside bargain products of lower quality that could potentially convey the wrong message to customers. There are also choices to be made about the distribution intensity (mass distribution) and the channel integration (multi-channel, which is the combination of different channels used to deliver the product).

Selecting the right distribution channel is a strategic issue, as some distribution routes will provide competitive benefits over others and will also meet the organization's strategic objectives more closely. The choice of channel will reflect the brand values and support the rest of the marketing mix. For example, if the product is of intermediate quality, priced at a discount, and promoted through sales promotions, customers would expect to find it in multiple retail outlets, discount stores, or to be available via the internet. Organizations which do not pay attention to where their products are distributed may be missing a source of competitive advantage, for example by selecting a channel that is being ignored by their competitors; or by selecting a channel that has just become available due to new technology, for example Amazon's recent announcement about Prime Air making remote deliveries using drones.

The product may pass directly from the supplier to the consumer, but many producers do not sell directly to consumers and will employ different types of intermediary to get the product where it needs to be. Intermediaries can take several forms. The most common are retail outlets or premises where goods and services are delivered to consumers, but intermediaries can also be wholesalers, agents, brokers, or distributors. However, every extra 'pair of hands' that the product moves through adds another level of cost to the final price. Marketers also have to decide whether to use push or pull strategies to affect their distribution channels. A push strategy is where marketing employs its sales team to encourage retailers to stock, promote, and actively sell their product range so that customers will be attracted by the easy availability of the product. This marketing technique works well with low involvement products and impulse buys. A pull strategy involves promoting the offer to the customers so that they go into retail spaces to request the products, which in turn encourages the retailer to stock more product. This technique is more effective with high involvement products and where there is high brand loyalty.

It is necessary to employ intermediaries to access some markets, such as the use of agents or partner retailers to access complicated markets like China. The use of intermediaries removes some of the logistical issues in getting products to customers who can be geographically dispersed, or who are purchasing in small numbers. Intermediaries (such as Booker wholesalers who supply independent retailers and caterers) also add value to the customer's purchasing experience, as they can contribute specialist knowledge, convenience, speed of service, sales staff, and advice, as well as increasing the accessibility of the product to the customer. Product positioning decisions have to be made about the number and types of channel selected, how many intermediaries are required. Service offers can also move through intermediaries such as travel agents or online agents, but the variables used to select the type of intermediary utilized will depend on how long the customer is willing to wait, how far they are willing to travel, and what level of service is required.

The development of the internet has added another channel for suppliers to use. Internet sites that provide a retail function, such as Amazon, eBay and Alibaba, allow products to be viewed, prices to be compared and products to be distributed widely. The development of internet sellers led to a danger that other types of intermediary could be eliminated from the marketplace. The delivery of goods bought over the internet still relies on carriers like DHL and Hermes to put the goods into the hands of the consumer, which has led to some consumers experiencing problems with the speed and reliability of delivery and delivery errors. Another disadvantage of internet purchasing is that customers still need to see, test, and handle certain products to check on their quality and functionality before purchase. This is why most internet companies will offer a 'no quibble' returns policy for products purchased through their website.

Finally, the anonymity of many internet sellers creates issues with trust on the part of purchasers. In the past, traditional intermediaries have added value to the purchase experience by developed a trusting relationship with their customers over time, but with the growth of internet shopping new techniques for developing trust have emerged, including the growth of independent sites such as Trust Pilot that encourages online posts of customer feedback on specific retailers. Online sites should strive to provide clear and accurate descriptions, offer secure online payments, and make it easier to return unwanted items to help to build trust.

Methods of distribution

One of the major decisions to be made about 'Place' is whether to use mass, selective, or exclusive distribution (see Figure 15) and how many levels of intermediaries are required to move the product efficiently from producer to customer. Mass distribution is where the product is sent through intermediaries with a broad market appeal, such as supermarkets, convenience stores, cash and carry outlets and internet sellers, such as Amazon. How these

Mass distribution

Example: Food products and toiletries

Selective distribution

Example: Televisions and home appliances

Exclusive distribution

Example: Luxury automobiles and prestige clothing

15. Methods of distribution.

outlets are supplied will depend on the product type and the quantity of products being delivered.

The Coca-Cola corporation provides an example of mass distribution, as their soft drinks are distributed in every conceivable way and to every possible place. They are available in draught, bottled, or canned form and from all types of retail outlet, restaurants, self-service machines, cafés, and hotels. Without this comprehensive distribution network, Coca-Cola would sell a fraction of the product that it does today. Selective distribution is where the supplier may choose to supply through a specific type of outlet. For example, televisions and other electrical goods are widely available through a limited number of retail outlets and department stores, where the sales personnel have the specialist knowledge to be able to assist the customer with their choice, although selective distribution has changed drastically with the growth of online retailers.

Exclusive distribution is where the supplier chooses to distribute through one type of intermediary only. The advantage of this approach is that the supplier obtains the greatest control over distribution and they can work closely with the intermediary to add value through their service provision. The exclusivity agreement may restrict the retailer to only stocking the supplier's product, or products of a similar quality. For some offers the exclusivity agreement may also include the rights to serve a particular geographic area or use their brand name. Porsche cars are found in exclusive retail environments, with bright lighting, well-trained and knowledgeable sales staff, free refreshments, and an exclusive atmosphere, all of which convey the brand's value and support their premium pricing. The supplier will only allow trained staff to supply their products to the consumer, and they generally select the retailer carefully, so that they can directly control how the product is presented to the customer.

Multi-channel and omni-channel distribution

Multi-channel distribution is where the supplier chooses to have their products available through a range of channels (see Figure 16). This is different from mass distribution, as multi-channel distribution is where a single producer uses all available channels of distribution to reach potential customers and improve their customer experience. Multi-channel distribution has been developed in response to customers switching channels to gain the best offer. Channel switching is where customers consider a range

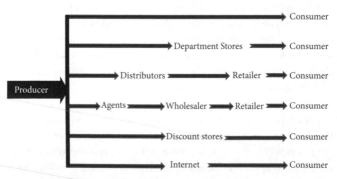

16. An example of multi-channel distribution.

of channels from which to purchase the product and select the one that is most convenient and economic to them. Alternatively, customers may have previously purchased from a local store, but then switch to a discount or warehouse outlet, or an online retailer, once they have made a product selection. The greater availability of comparative information about the offers that can be purchased from different distribution channels is probably increasing channel switching. In response, suppliers are trying to cover all possible distribution options to ensure that they get the sale.

A number of consumer producers/suppliers have adopted what is called an omni-channel approach. This is where the suppliers aim to improve their customers' user experience by working in parallel with various distribution channels and linking this activity with their marketing communications and other supporting resources. The omni-channel approach supersedes the multi-channel approach, as it integrates different types of channel with e-commerce, social media, and mobile applications, so that they reinforce positive messages about the product's availability. Early examples of omni-channel distribution are found in financial services and telecommunications industries, where the customer is able to engage with the supplier through multiple avenues to gain product information and advice before making a purchase. The effect is to remove stress from making the purchase decision and provide a more enjoyable and efficient purchase experience.

There are important differences regarding the structure of the distribution channels between consumer, industrial, and service markets. Consumer channels tend to be longer and more involved due to the nature of the products. Industrial or B2B products are more likely to be delivered directly from the producer to the customer, because the quantities purchased are usually larger and the number of customers fewer. B2B customers also expect a degree of expert knowledge about the products they are purchasing and information on how the purchase will benefit their business. Service channels are also more likely to be direct, although they may include the use of agents or franchise providers, because a service is inseparable from its provider and it needs to be delivered by someone who understands the offer and is able to provide it in the right way. An example may be purchasing theatre tickets, which may be obtained direct from the theatre, through a ticket agent, or online.

All 'place' decisions are made to reflect the amount of control that is required in the delivery of the product to the customer. Vehicle fuel is delivered on forecourts that are designed to ensure that the product is delivered safely and accurately into the purchasers' vehicles. As this is a hazardous product its delivery is tightly controlled by the supplier. The same can be said for the delivery of medical supplies, which are generally supplied through registered pharmacists. Further, the service delivery of medical advice is only available from registered practitioners. However, the development of the internet has disrupted many service industries that deliver this type of specialist information, because they provide additional access to knowledge and an alternative form of provision.

Chapter 7
Product, new product development, and service marketing

Physical goods and services are offered to the customer as part of the exchange relationship. The generic product (goods or services) is what the organization provides to their customers to generate money by satisfying their needs. The product can be configured or manipulated to meet the needs of various target customer groups and is therefore a fundamental part of the marketing mix. The concept of the product lifecycle helps marketers to decide how and when to market various products to different target groups, and to decide when the offer needs to be refreshed or repositioned in the marketplace. Therefore, we will explore the function and importance of new product development (NPD), how and when existing products are replaced with an improved offer.

The divide between goods and services is not a hard one, as marketers can add service attributes to physical product offers and service offers rely on physical attributes to distinguish their offer from competitors, so we will explore the differences between marketing services and marketing physical goods. A service is characterized as being intangible, perishable, variable, and inseparable from its production, and these aspects of service are linked to the augmented marketing mix, or the seven Ps. Employing the seven Ps means that there are extra marketing tools available to distinguish and communicate their offer to the customer. The problem that exists with service marketing is that it is not possible to market intangibles, so marketers have to rely on tangible clues to convey the value of the offer to the customer. For example, airlines will talk about the number of destinations they cover, the age of the aircraft, and the amount of space between seats, but avoid mentioning the quality of the service or the food. The necessity of differentiating the product offer from those of competitors has led to many organizations offering a combination of physical products and services to enhance their offer.

What is a product?

The product is the offer that is made to customers and clients. If it does not provide the function, benefits, and value that the customer requires it will not be successful. Some products are simple goods, like potatoes. The potato is a basic food, and beyond the different varieties that are available, one Maris Piper potato looks very like another, so that the suppliers of Maris Pipers (farmers) emphasize the benefits of purchasing the generic product, rather than their own particular offer. This product is a commodity as there is a market price and a general standard of acceptable quality. The potatoes are sold in bulk through mass markets and the suppliers do not differentiate their offers. More complex products, and most service offers, can be marketed on their specific functions, benefits, and values, so that one offer can be differentiated from others in the market. To achieve differentiation, marketers can look at three aspects of the product: its core functions, the formal aspects (sometimes called the actual product), and the augmented product (see Figure 17).

All aspects of a product must fit with the target customer's needs in order to maximize sales. Marketers are able to alter aspects of the core, formal, or augmented product. Let us take a microwave oven as an example. The core product is the electrical oven that heats food, and it must perform this function effectively if it is to be purchased. However, a microwave may be produced with or

Augmented Product is the additional customer service, after-sales support, guarantees, installation or credit that accompany the product

Formal Product is the features, brand values, quality, design, and packaging of the product.

Core Product comprises the benefits and functionality that the product brings to the customers.

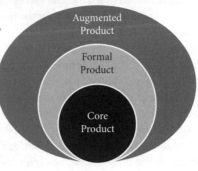

17. **Constituents of a product.**

without a turntable, in different colours and designs, at differing levels of quality, and with or without a brand name. These are all aspects of the formal or actual product as they are part of the product, but they are not essential to its basic function of heating food. The augmented product comprises the things (often services) that can be added to enhance the attractiveness of the offer, such as a one- or two-year guarantee, special delivery service, installation, a service contract, and after-sales support. Each of the formal and augmented offers will be included in various combinations depending on the requirements of the target segment.

The same sort of marketing techniques can be used with service offers. Taking car insurance as an example, the core product will be the guarantee that the service provider will cover any loss or damage that occurs over a specified time, as outlined in the service contract. The formal product will be the different combinations of benefits that the contract can include, such as a courtesy car, named drivers, fully comprehensive cover, or multiple car cover. The augmented product would be the extras that can be included that do not affect the basic offer, such as a protected no claims discount, insurance cover for items being transported in the car, or the ability to cover other drivers temporarily using the vehicle.

Philip Kotler extended the three levels of product to five to provide a greater number of elements for the marketer to use. To the core and formal (or generic in his model) and augmented products, Kotler added the 'expected' product and the 'potential' product. The 'expected' product comprises the additional benefits that the product should confer if a specific product offer is selected, such as the ability to 'grill' the food in our microwave example. The potential product is more about the benefits that could be accrued in the future if a specific product is selected, such as reliability and durability. By marketing these additional aspects of product, the marketer can differentiate their offer from the competition.

The product portfolio

The majority of larger organizations will manage a number of product lines and often supply several markets. This is called their product portfolio or product mix. An organization will usually develop an initial product which is successful, and then they will create associated products to broaden the range, or to increase the depth of the product line. Increasing the depth of the product line means that the company will offer more products that perform the same function in different ways, for example Procter & Gamble offer a range of shampoos to the market for men or women, and for different hair types. Increasing the product portfolio's width means servicing a variety of customers with a wider range of products, which spreads the organization's risk in case their original product's sales start to decline. Procter & Gamble, for example, provide not only shampoos, but also other personal cleansing products (such as toothpaste and face creams), cosmetics, and cleaning products (kitchen cleaners and washing products).

Increasing the width and depth of their product portfolio reduces the risk of putting all their effort into servicing a single market, but it also increases the complexity of managing the product mix. To help marketers to decide which products and product lines to

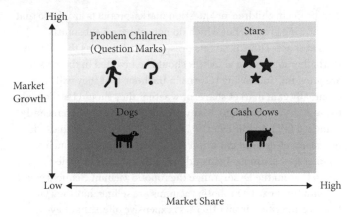

18. The BCC matrix or Boston box.

support, the Boston Consulting Company (BCC) developed a
diagnostic model (see Figure 18).

Each of the products or product lines that the organization
produces is measured in terms of their market share and rate of
market growth. The products with the greatest relative market
share and market growth are placed in the 'Stars' box. These are
the products that will require the most marketing effort, as they
have the greatest potential to provide future sales revenue.
Dyson's 'stars' could be their room fans, which have been selling
very well and their market share is still growing. Marketers
should always support their stars to help them to keep on
growing and by making sure that the product's offer is still
relevant to the target customer groups. The products with the
greatest market share but slow growth are placed in the 'cash
cows' quadrant. These products have already achieved their
optimum place in the market and are likely to continue to sell
well supported only by maintenance marketing. Taking the
example from Dyson's product range, their cordless vacuum
cleaners could fall into this category.

The 'problem children' or 'question marks' products are those that are showing growth, but which do not yet have a substantial market share. These products present a challenge, as the dilemma is whether marketing activities should be invested in them as they are providing increasing returns in the hope that they will eventually gain market share, or whether they should be allowed to grow at their own rate. Many products that have been recently launched fall into this category, as well as those that perhaps do not have a clear differentiation from their competitors, such as another new shampoo being added to this already crowded market. From the Dyson range the robotic vacuum cleaners could fall into this box. The robotic vacuums are selling, but they face fierce competition from other less expensive offers that have a greater market share.

Finally, the products that have low market share and falling market growth ('dogs') present a different marketing challenge. These products are likely to be at the end of their lifecycle (see section below), but they are still providing revenue with minimum marketing effort, such as Dyson's corded vacuum cleaners (they have already announced that they do not intend to develop this range further). Additionally, they may have to be kept in the product mix if they represent a product that supports another product line, such as the books in a series that are not popular, but which complete the set. The Boston box is a useful tool, but one that needs to be used in conjunction with other market information, so that decisions can be made about 'dogs' being either discontinued or invested in to move them into another box; 'problem children' invested in to become 'stars', or dropped as they are too expensive to develop; and how much and what type of marketing support 'cash cows' and 'stars' need to remain successful.

Product lifecycle

The concept of the product lifecycle is helpful in identifying how to market a product group over time. The basic idea is that all

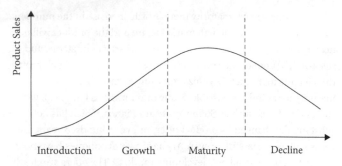

19. The product lifecycle.

products go through the same stages of launch or introduction of
the new offer to the market, growth, maturity, decline, and if
appropriate rejuvenation (see Figure 19).

When the product is first introduced (launched) into the market it
will need to have the most attractive combination of core, formal,
and augmented aspects of the product for the target group. It will
need to be priced competitively, be available appropriately, and
have considerable support from marketing promotions to raise
awareness in the minds of the target customers. For example,
when smart phones were first introduced, they were heavily
promoted to the target segment and only a limited range of
options were supplied. During the second stage of growth the
product will be expected to appeal to a wider range of customers
and so will require some of the formal and augmented aspects to
be adjusted to differentiate the offer from competitors and attract
new customer groups. Promotions will still remain high and have
a wider scope, while the pricing and place may be adjusted for the
new customer groups. This is when the product should start to
become profitable for the organization, but how quickly this
happens will depend on the pricing strategy selected at launch.
Demand for smart phones grew quickly and other suppliers joined
the market, forcing the original suppliers to reduce their prices
and provide a greater range of options and extra features.

When products reach maturity there is little increase in the numbers sold, but they still have a high market share and the product will not need the same amount of promotion, the prices will be stable, and sales of this product will contribute more to the organization's profits than it costs to market. Organizations aim to keep their products in maturity for as long as possible. Some organizations have been very successful at this, such as Steinway Grand Pianos, which has not substantially changed its product offer for over a hundred years, and yet is still as successful as ever. Arguably, smart phones have now reached maturity in all but developing markets. The offers are clearly differentiated, and each supplier has an established market share. Marketing is at maintenance levels unless there is some new option or feature to be promoted. Extending the product lifecycle can be achieved through increased investment in promotions and rebranding, by adding new features and packaging, or by targeting new customer groups by promoting a different use of the product. However, the majority of products eventually (or quite quickly for fad products) experience declining sales. This decline is created by changing customer needs and by NPD. At this point, the product will either need to be rejuvenated (totally redesigned and relaunched) if it is going to be continued or moved to a lower price point.

New product development

It is said that if an organization does not innovate it will not remain in business because the market environment is continuously changing as developing technologies provide new opportunities and customers' expectations change. The majority of organizations will engage with incremental innovation, which is where relatively small changes are continuously made to products and services in response to customers' feedback and competitors' activities to maintain products' popularity. However, NPD is more radical, and some innovations can reshape the whole market and challenge the competition because they offer something fundamentally different, such as Dyson vacuum cleaners. As a result, David Jobber identified four broad categories for NPD:

Product Development

Marmite have extented their product range by adding new variants

20. Marmite line extensions.

1. 'Product replacements' or upgrades to the existing offer. This would be incremental changes to the existing product lines as already discussed. This type of NPD represents around 45 per cent of the total number of new products offered to the market.
2. 'Additions' to existing lines, which is where a successful product line such as Marmite is developed to provide new and interesting variants (see Figure 20). This type of NPD represents around 25 per cent of the total.
3. 'New product' lines are where organizations develop new products that extend their expertise into different markets or industries. For example, Dyson has built on his successful cyclone vacuum cleaners by developing hand dryers, bladeless air fans, and hair dryers. This NPD represents around 20 per cent of the total.
4. 'New to the world' products are those that disrupt the existing offers to the market. Usually based in new technologies and techniques, 'new to the world' products change the market itself by offering new functions, features, and benefits to customers. An example would be the introduction of mobile phones, and then the development of smart phones. This type of NPD accounts for up to 10 per cent of the total.

Whichever type of NPD is undertaken the process is time-consuming and costly. Most organizations will have an R&D department that will be responsible for keeping up with the latest developments in the field and coming up with new ideas. However, not all NPD ideas will be taken to commercialization and most organizations will have an established process for developing new products, such as the NPD funnel or the 'stage and gate' process, which is where distinct development stages or phases are separated by a series of decision points known as gates. Continuation through each gate will be made by a management or steering committee that will make decisions based on forecasts, risk analyses, resource requirements, and the overall business case for each project.

At the start of the NPD processes a number of original ideas for new products are generated to meet the organization's new product objectives and strategy—which customer needs are they trying to meet? The initial ideas are then screened for viability by presenting the product's concept to a group of representative customers and then analysing them for practicality—does the organization have the necessary resources for production and is there a potential market for the offer? The analysis stage of the process will also include a cost benefit analysis and break-even analysis to check that the product is financially viable. Many products are rejected in the initial screening and analysis stages, so that the number of ongoing projects is significantly reduced.

The next two parts of the process are the development of prototypes and test marketing. Many NPD projects fail at this stage as they are either too difficult or not cost effective to manufacture or the test marketing reveals flaws in their conceptualization. The last part of the process consists of putting together a commercialization package (developing a value proposition and strategy of how the product will be marketed) and moving into full production. Although there is an 'urban legend' that as many as 80 to 90 per cent of NPD projects result in failure, researchers George Castellion and Stephen Markham established that the actual number is nearer 40 to 50 per cent failure of commercialized projects. However, this is still a high percentage, and the total number of new, fully commercialized products per annum is quite small.

Once the new product is launched its acceptance by the market is still not guaranteed, despite all the testing and market research. If the new product is a variant or a replacement for an existing product, the customer may not be willing to accept the changes and may move to a competitor's offer. If it is a new product line, customers may feel that there is no requirement for it. If the offer is 'new to the world' then the producer runs the risk that the market will not understand the new features and benefits or simply will not want them.

Customers called 'innovators' are usually keen to try any 'new to market' products (around 2.5 per cent of the target segment). They like to try new products out and discuss their experiences on social media and in the press. Marketers hope that these innovators will attract the attention of 'early adopters' (around 13.5 per cent of the target segment) who are the group of customers that are open to new ideas and are adventurous, but who do not like to take too many risks. The 'early majority' (around 34 per cent of the target segment) will wait until the 'early adopters' have tried the product out before they try it for themselves. The 'late majority' (around 34 per cent of the target segment) wait until it looks as if the product has been successful before adopting it, and the 'laggards' (around 16 per cent of the target segment) are those who eventually try out the new offer once it has become established.

Product strategy

In order to understand how organizations are able to expand their product mix, Igor Ansoff developed his growth matrix. The basic premise is that there are four options when considering market/product growth strategies: penetration, market development, product development, and diversification. The first option is to penetrate the existing market more deeply by configuring the product more closely to the target customer's needs and beating the competition through better promotions, distribution, and pricing. For example, Marmite (a Unilever product) has recently engaged in new television advertising and point of sale promotions to increase sales to their customer base. The second option is to find new markets for the existing products. This would involve promotions to a new group of customers either within the existing market (new usage) or in a new market, perhaps overseas. The promotions should explain how the existing product could meet the new customer's needs, and the product will need to be priced appropriately and its distribution through new channels negotiated. Marmite has been marketed to new territories such as India.

The third option is to engage in NPD to deepen the product line or its width to find new offers that will attract the existing target customers to buy more variants of the product. An example of this can be seen in Figure 20, which shows that the Marmite brand has increased their offer to their existing market through line extensions. The new products will need support from promotions such as taste tests, advertising, and social media campaigns to increase awareness, but the distribution channels are likely to be similar to those of the original product.

The final quadrant contains the riskiest growth option, which is to develop a new product for a new market or group of customers, called 'diversification'. Diversification has not been attempted by Marmite but was successfully carried out by Dyson when they expanded from their vacuum cleaner product lines to include products such as room fans, hair dryers, and hand dryers. The customers for hand dryers are not necessarily the same as those for vacuum cleaners, as the main customer base for hand dryers would be B2B.

Marketing services

Most of the previous section has been focused on marketing physical products or goods, but there are some specific features of services that need to be considered separately. Evert Gummersson, a Scandinavian academic, outlined that service is an integral part of the value proposition, as value is created during the customers' interaction with the supplier during the consumption process. Pure service offers such as insurance, financial services, and other professional services are all intangible, inseparable from the provider, variable, and perishable. The intangibility of the service provides the greatest challenge to marketing because the service cannot be touched, there is no way of accurately standardizing a service, it cannot be patented, and the service is consumed when and where it is available. The intangibility of the service influences the other elements of inseparability, variability, and perishability as the benefits of the service can only be experienced when the customer is interacting with the provider. Consequently, the original marketing mix of product, price, place, and promotion needed to be adapted to convey the quality of a specific service experience to customers. Bernard Booms and Mary Bitner, who developed the concept of the seven Ps, suggested that the additional three marketing Ps of customer service (people), the selling environment and documentation (physical evidence), and service processes (process) should be included for service marketing.

As services are *intangible*, the product cannot be configured in the same way as a physical good, so service products are sold as a total product concept that is comprised of a combination of tangible and intangible aspects (see Figure 21). The service will still be sold on its core service (obtaining a haircut) and its formal elements (added products such as conditioner or hair spray) and augmented elements (a supportive cup of tea or coffee), as mentioned above. Additionally, the hair salon may have physical

21. The goods vs services continuum.

elements on display that may denote service quality, such as certificates of quality or written recommendations, and/or luxury seating and air conditioning. Consequently, physical evidence, especially those aspects of the service that rely on the five senses of taste, sight, smell, sound, and touch, must be carefully managed to convey the overall quality of the offer.

As services are *inseparable from the provider*, the channel of distribution is usually more direct than for physical goods, but services may still be delivered in a physical environment that can be configured to provide an appropriate level of comfort or sophisticated expertise to reflect the service quality offered, such as banking halls, hair salons, or airport lounges. Service providers will also influence the perception of quality of their service through their brand reputation. Service brands should be distinctive, memorable, relevant, and flexible, but it is critical that they deliver the promises that they make. However good the organization is in delivering their brand values, it is still not possible to ensure that every customer receives the same level of satisfaction from the service, as each customer has their own individual perspective on what is an acceptable, satisfactory, and excellent level of service. As a result, a service is classed as *variable* at the point of delivery. Finally, services are *perishable*, which means that they cannot be stored for later use. An example may be a restaurant service. Part of the service offer is to provide freshly cooked food that will need to be consumed when it is served, or it will be spoilt.

Promoting service products is more difficult than promoting goods, as the customer's experience can vary with every interaction. Consequently, word of mouth and social media reviews are critical to the success of service promotions. Additionally, comparison sites such as TripAdvisor can provide a wide range of opinions that help the customer to make their choice and provide reliable information on the service experience. These elements all relate back to the standard of service provided by the people delivering it. People are the human actors that are involved in the exchange, between the service provider and the customer. The service providers are critical as they are representing the organization and should convey its values during the interaction, such as British Airways cabin crew, in the way that they dress, converse, and interact with the traveller.

Service providers can be influenced through training on how to deliver the service to meet the organization's needs. However, Adrian Furnham and Rebecca Milner identified that there are likely to be many personal elements (such as tiredness, mood, job-related stress, and the effects of previous interactions or incidents) that affect the interaction between the individual customer and the service provider, which makes the 'people' element particularly difficult to control. For example, the visitor to a hair salon may have had a difficult day or be unsure what they want from the service provider, resulting in them being hard to communicate with and the hairdresser not being able to deliver a satisfactory service. Alternatively, the hairdresser may have been very busy and be suffering from job-related stress, which may make them less attentive than they should be. Advertising can still be used to convey the value of the service and the range of services that are performed, but the aim of service promotions is to get the potential customer to engage with the service provider and it is their experience that will affect whether customers support the advertising messages in social media or not.

The third service element that should be managed by marketing is process, in other words how the customer is attracted to the offer and guided through the stages of purchasing and consumption. The customer should experience engaging with the service in an acceptable, logical, and satisfying way. Events should happen in an expected order and the supporting documentation should be provided at the appropriate time. Two of the key processes are booking the service and then paying for it. The booking may depend on the quality of the website or the booking agent. Pricing services does usually conform to the same pricing mechanisms as those for physical goods, although the timing of payment can be a variable in the service provision. For example, payment may be made before, during, or after the service has been received. Some payments can be made by instalments to extend the period of service provision, such as for insurance or gardening services. Some services may have price restrictions placed on them by governments or professional codes including health services, such as opticians and dental services, and therefore the prices charged will be controlled. Many services can also experience differential pricing, where the cost of the service will vary depending on the time of day or the location of the provision, for example train and airline services charge at different rates depending on when you travel.

The three extra Ps of the marketing mix indicate how critical people are in the provision and marketing of services. People are the link between the service organization and the customers, so how the service is perceived in the marketplace will depend on each individual interaction. Consequently, however effective an organization is in managing their service elements, the service's value will be determined by their customers' experiences and their feedback to the service provider and through social media.

Chapter 8
The changing nature of marketing

Organizations do not operate in a vacuum; they interact with the surrounding environment, respond to its stimulus, and strive to influence their customers' attitudes and behaviours. Marketing plays a boundary-spanning role for the organization, as it interacts directly with customers and provides intelligence about changes in the marketplace. As a consequence, decisions about marketing strategy play a crucial role in business success, as organizations struggle to meet the increasingly complex needs of their customers, society as a whole, and new technology, while still needing to differentiate their offer from that of their competitors. However, nothing has been more transforming to the function of marketing than the development of the internet, digitalization, and, more recently, artificial intelligence (AI).

The growth of social media has provided new opportunities for communicating and establishing relationships with customers and consumers. These opportunities are considerably more flexible than traditional media and offer the possibility of focusing on different markets and targeting existing audiences in a new way. Sites such as Facebook not only offer an innovative advertising channel, but also a platform for interacting with customers to help organizations to improve their offers, gain ideas for new products, and find additional customer groups. However, the ability of customers to publicly comment on the product or service experience that they have had means that marketers are no longer totally in control of their marketing messages and are struggling to guide the public's perception of their brand and product offerings. Consequently, many marketing departments are striving to understand which of their activities are controllable and which are not.

With the growth of service industries in mature economies, the internet and other technological developments have provided the perfect conditions for driving the rapid growth of tech start-ups, media-based businesses, and e-commerce. Tech-based, virtual businesses such as Scopic Software and Buffer are often small or micro-businesses (run by a few people) which are creating the need for the development of new business models and imaginative marketing techniques. The growth of the public visibility of organizations' actions has led to the need to increase transparency and for a greater focus on organizations communicating their ethical position. Societal marketing, where businesses can highlight how their activities are benefiting society as a whole, has developed in response to concerns for organizations to be visibly ethical as well as meeting customers' needs. Internet connectivity offers the opportunity for marketers to operate globally, without physical restrictions, but this presents another challenge to maintaining their ethical integrity.

Influences of social media

The development of social media is offering marketers another route to market and a different way of engaging with potential customers (see Chapter 5). Social media platforms, such as Twitter, Weibo, Wechat, Baidu, Snapchat, Instagram, QQ or QZone, Tumblr, and Facebook, are mostly used by participants for expressing their opinions and showcasing events in their lives, so that they can be shared with friends and other interested parties. Critically the content of social media is provided by the participants, with interest groups and internet communities starting up spontaneously around different topics. It is the ability of social media to facilitate participants' engagement with any topic that allows marketers to use this medium to convey information about their products. Marketers have also realized that combining social media marketing with traditional marketing messages creates an interactive and valuable experience for their customers.

Start-up companies in particular begin by 'showcasing' their offer to customers via various posts and opinions, creating interest through online word of mouth promotion. This initial action encourages their customers to share their opinions about the ways in which they have used or experienced various products. Once the social networks have been established organizations can use effective social media marketing to create closer relationships with customers, encouraging them to share their preferences and interests, and become part of the organization's loyal community, such as Dunkin' Donuts or Harley-Davidson. Marketers are able to purchase internet advertising slots linked to topics of interest. Facilities such as Google Ad words, a pay-per-click advertising method, also allow marketers to create and run adverts on Google. Organizations are able to optimize search engine results by editing content and HTML and associated coding to highlight specific key words to make sure that they appear near the top of a search engine listing for customers who are looking for particular products. Backing up social media marketing with more traditional (but still online) advertising is critical to maintaining visibility.

Tech start-up companies are run by those who aim to bring new offers to market through technology, such as Just-Eat, Deliveroo, or Uber. They not only market their company online; they also run their organization and deliver their content virtually. These tech companies provide a platform where fast-food restaurants with delivery services can register their offer, and the clients can go to the platform to order and pay for their food, which is then delivered directly to the customer.

Social media marketing can also take the form of posted blogs, social and micro blogs (allowing users to exchange small elements of contents), wikis, podcasts, pictures, and vlogs (video blogs), as well as participating on rating sites. The aim is to make use of these activities to advertise their business, and organizations are able to perform integrated marketing activities with retailers, suppliers, digital services, and participate in events and discussions at a much lower cost than through traditional marketing media. Large corporations, advocacy groups, political parties, charities, and established brands have been quick to capitalize on the advantages of social media. An investigation into the effects of social media marketing on luxury fashion brands by Angela Kim and Eunju Ko identified that it can increase the organization's customer value, relationship value, and brand values with their target customers, and increase the customers' purchase intention. Burberry, the UK fashion icon, has recently used the social media sites of Twitter, Pinterest, and YouTube to refresh its fashion heritage image by adding a contemporary twist, thereby targeting a younger demographic. What is clear is that organizations that do not engage in marketing through social media are ignoring an opportunity to reach new customer groups and uncover new trends in customers' needs.

Digitization and the marketing mix

Digitization makes it possible to organize data through software programs to create marketing knowledge and make the information accessible. The increased use of the internet by customers is generating more data that can be captured through webpages, cookies, and loyalty programmes, which can be interrogated to uncover more customer insights. 'Big data' is the generic term for data held nationally and internationally. Data is held on customers' purchasing behaviours, internet searches, web complaints, and usage of the organization's products reported on social media. It is collected during online interactions through web-linked devices (the Internet of Things). The grocery retailer Tesco is able to link the data from their loyalty cards with purchasing data from their tills and searches made by their customers on their website. Analysing this big data from the Internet of Things enables Tesco to build up a detailed picture of their customers' preferences and to personalize offers and adjust promotions to their needs. Turning this super-large amount of data into usable information is achieved by interrogating these complex, linked datasets.

The marketing mix can still be employed to target customer groups effectively, but now the digital component has to be considered. Take the 'product' part of the marketing mix as an example. If the organization is selling a physical product it can be communicated 'virtually' on the organization's website, where its image can be manipulated to suit the customer's needs. For example, some furniture manufacturers, such as SofaSofa, provide customers with the ability to 'see' their selected product (a sofa) online in different designs, fabrics, and colours before placing their order. This feature is as valuable to the customer as going into an outlet and testing how comfortable the sofa is to sit on, as they can visualize the product in their own sitting room.

Service offers are made more 'tangible' through advertising and imaging on the organization's website, as features and available options and benefits can be explained, and customer recommendations provided. Customers can also configure the offer to meet their needs so that they feel more engaged with this intangible offer. Travel agents have been performing these interactions and personalization functions for the travel industry for many years, through the use of brochures and face-to-face interactions with the customer. Now many of these types of transactions are conducted through web-platforms, which are more convenient for their customers, as well as cheaper and less time-consuming for the travel company to operate.

Digitalization has put retailers under greater pressure to provide their offers on the internet, driven by the growth of competition from e-retailers such as Amazon and Alibaba. Using the internet to obtain products means that customers can have much greater input into when and how delivery is made. This increased customization of delivery can be very valuable to customers, and its provision is generally considered to be more cost effective to run, as the organization does not have to cover the overheads for multiple physical outlets or use retailers to reach their customers. It should be noted, however, that e-retailers do not entirely remove the costs of selling and delivering physical products as they do have transportation costs and the cost of handling returns and/or complaints if there are issues with the quality of the products. What the internet has done for 'place' is to improve access and thereby increase the number of channels available for customers to obtain their products (see Chapter 6).

Service products can, of course, be provided and distributed totally through the internet. Music and films are just as likely to be purchased online, in the form of digital files, as they are to be purchased as physical CDs or DVDs. Many service offers can be configured so that they are obtainable on- or offline, most retailers will now offer both 'brick and click' options. Banking activities, for example, can be provided completely online, although access to their services are still available through high street branches. Management consultants can operate remotely through internet interactions and video conferencing, as well as by visiting their clients to review operations personally.

Pricing may also be adjusted by the increased use of technology, for example through the development of dynamic pricing where prices fluctuate continuously. Dynamic pricing can be influenced by the consumer's online interactions, such as the time of day that the product is viewed or purchased, how many times the product is viewed, if there is a sudden increase in demand, or even when the organization realizes that it needs to increase the rate of sales, so they repeatedly run especially low prices for short periods. It is not so easy to make these price adjustments in a retail space in the same dynamic way that can be achieved on the internet due to physical constraints and legal restrictions. The airline industry is an example of dynamic pricing in action, where online customers can benefit from continuously 'pricing' the cost of a proposed trip, until they find an offer that meets their needs. Of course, customers can also change elements of the trip, such as airline used, dates, or seating until they find the best offer for them. The open access provided by the internet also allows customers to search for items at certain price points (this is frequently seen in car sales), or they can search for best prices through comparison sites.

The 'promotions' part of the mix can also be reconfigured with digital content in mind. As mentioned in the section above, the great advantage of promotions that are run through websites and social media is the ability to generate a two-way conversation with customers. Advertisements, webinars, and other offer-related content and public relation materials can be included in posts, blogs, and on search engine sites, as well as on the company website. The result is that the digital marketing mix offers greater opportunity to personalize offers, personal interactions, and content for individual customers.

The process part of the marketing mix has been transformed through the development of new technology and the internet. How the customer is moved through the buying journey can now be handled either on- or offline, or by a combination of the two. Even the simplest of purchases are likely to include some type of e-processes. Customers buying from fast-food outlets will enter the outlet, select their order (an order they can place online prior to arrival), and go to the till, where they are then likely to be offered the opportunity to pay either via the internet or in cash. These customers may then take part in a customer survey or some marketing research through the internet as part of the post-purchase evaluation. As mentioned above, physical evidence of the offers can be provided through web-platforms, where the customer can be reassured of the product's quality, provided with operating/process information, and taken through any registration documents required.

Changing buyer–seller relationships

Further changes to the marketing environment include the growth in the power of retailers over the market, changing customer behaviours and internationalization. The purchasing power of large retailers such as Walmart, Saks Fifth Avenue, Amazon, and Alibaba has put pressure on suppliers, including some of the largest organizations in the world, to adapt their processes, pricing, and distribution to meet retailers' needs. Supermarkets, for example, have been accused of being so prescriptive about the products they will stock and prices that they will accept from suppliers that the selling organizations have had to either adapt or withdraw from the relationship. This alteration in the buyer–seller relationship has resulted in marketers no longer 'marketing to' their B2B customers but having to 'market with' them (co-marketing), such as Dell computers promoting their offer with Intel. The result is that marketers need to know more about the retailer's customers (the consumers) so that they are able to create a marketing mix that will appeal to both the retailer and the consumer.

The relationship with large powerful retailers is one of the responsibilities of the 'sales' team and has resulted in the development of specialist salespeople (such as key account managers) who are able to build integrated relationships with these large customers. Salespeople will need new skills, dedicated resources, and support from technology to enable them to manage the customer experience. All the organization's marketing/sales activities will need to be engaged to manage every touchpoint across the customer's journey to purchase, so that the brand themes and value proposition are aligned in a seamless transition, both on- and offline. The touchpoints are where the organization interacts with the customer in the customer's journey and cover the pre-purchase, purchase, and post-purchase phases.

The salesperson should be able to guide their customers through the purchasing phase by configuring the marketing mix to their requirements and the requirements of their consumers. Not only do organizations have to review their experiences with consumers, it is also now necessary for them to review the performance of their products and brands with the buyers. There is now an additional role for salespeople, as they develop a deeper customer understanding and greater creativity. They need to digitally communicate the brand's values and product benefits both informally and formally to individual consumers and consumer groups through social media. However, digital technologies will also be able to help the salesperson to gain this deeper customer understanding through behavioural analytics of the customers' digital interactions, but only as long as the analytical algorithms that are developed are able to keep up with the rapidly changing nature of the market.

Internationalization

The increasingly boundaryless nature of the world's markets also presents the marketer with some challenges in their buyer–seller interactions. With the development of the internet it no longer matters where the customer or the supplier is based. Marketing messages can be transmitted world-wide, and goods and some services can be delivered internationally (with the exception of some restricted goods). Multinational organizations, such as HSBC, P&G, Samsung, Google, Apple, and Toyota, employ global marketing activities in order to attract the maximum number of customers and configure their offers so that they are valuable to every market with which they engage. International marketers consequently have to achieve two things: a marketing strategy that is globally relevant and consistent with their brand values; and individual marketing mixes for territories that have specific characteristics and distinctive customer needs. For example, Unilever has an international brand strategy for each of its brands that conveys a globally consistent message about customer value, but they allow individual subsidiaries to configure their marketing activities to their local needs.

The key challenge of international marketing is to manage the risk of operating in territories that are unfamiliar to the organization. Marketing operates on accurate information, but it is sometimes difficult to gain the relevant information in overseas markets. Global organizations will carefully choose which markets to enter, and they may need to employ local marketing and salespeople to make sure that they are interacting with the overseas territory effectively. A simple example of how things can go wrong in an international context is when Nokia/Microsoft launched their new mobile phone 'Lumia' having failed to realize that this term is a Spanish slang word for 'prostitute'—potentially negatively affecting sales in Spanish-speaking territories.

When entering new markets, the price and distribution elements of the marketing mix will have to be adapted to local conditions due to currency exchange rates. Distribution will rely on the nature of the local infrastructure in terms of internet connectivity, road or rail quality, and their retail structure. However, the marketing communications and promotions, and product elements will either remain the same or will need some adjustment to make them appropriate to the local market (see Table 7).

Ethics in marketing

In line with many other areas of the organization's operations there has been a growing debate around ethics in marketing, especially with the development of social media and the internet.

Table 7. Locally adapted international marketing strategies

International marketing mix strategies	Same product	Adapted product	New product
Same marketing communications	The product is new to the local market, although the values and marketing messages remain the same as those to other markets	The product will need some adaptation to deliver the same values as existing offers, but the marketing messages remain the same	A new product is developed for the market in line with the values and marketing messages of existing offers made by the company
Adapted marketing communications	The same product is sold to the new market, but will need some adaptation to the marketing messages to be relevant	Both the product and marketing mix will need some adaptation to the local market	A new product is developed for the local market that delivers the same values as existing products, and the marketing messages are adjusted to meet local needs
New marketing communications	The same product is sold to the new market, but it will need new marketing messages to be appropriate for the local market	The product will need to be adapted, but new marketing messages will be needed to communicate with the local market appropriately	The product innovation for the local market requires customized marketing messages to communicate with the local market

The development of mass marketing and international communications provides marketers with the capacity to manipulate social values and perceptions in favour of their products, while they are being challenged to maintain general ethics of honesty and integrity in marketing messages. The advertising industry has been accused in the press of highlighting the inequalities in society by promoting the purchase of products that not everyone can afford; and failing to take into account societal health issues by promoting unhealthy products such as very sweet, sugar-laden snacks and drinks, or tobacco. The continued employment of super-thin models in the fashion industry has also raised concerns in the general public that the industry is potentially promoting destructive behaviours and a negative body image that could affect some vulnerable people.

The increased use of the internet and social media has thrown up more concerns around marketing activities. On occasions, the internet, television, and social media have been accused of displaying images that promote a kind of mass hysteria and 'group think' that have a greater geographical reach than previously. These exaggerated behaviours and the ability to comment about 'news items' have now become a social norm that some contributors are happy to exploit to drive their marketing messages to receptive audiences. There are various debates around the ethics of the personalization of marketing communications, in particular where online vlogs and blogs could constitute an invasion of privacy, exposing participants to social comment (sometimes destructive) and ridicule that can be detrimental to their mental health.

Leading researchers into the Internet of Things, Krystan ten Berg, Ton Spil, and Robin Effing, explored the privacy paradox (privacy vs personalization) and explained that as organizations capture data on users in order to provide new products, solutions, and services for the customer's benefit, they are also aggregating information on where people are located (through Wi-Fi tracking), recording their personal activities and personal data—all of which could constitute a security risk to the individual. There is also a growing concern about how personal data is shared, who it is shared with, and the use of machines (rather than people) to extract and evaluate the information gained from big data. However, the research has also revealed that highlighting the perceived benefits of interaction, reassurances about privacy, and the development of trust between the organization and individual can help to influence the customers' willingness to reveal personal information.

Consequently, all organizations, both public and private, are challenged to remain ethical in their marketing communications. To achieve this, marketers are adopting new marketing initiatives, tools, and techniques, such as societal marketing or using social media, vlogging, and blogging to engage interpersonally with people to help to 'humanize' their messages and set them in more socially acceptable contexts.

Societal marketing

Societal marketing has become important to organizations in response to changing perceptions of the market concerning ethics, corporate social responsibility, and sustainable development. Societal marketing is where social responsibility is combined with commercial marketing strategies so that a distinction is created between the immediate satisfaction generated for the customer and the direct benefits for the organization, compared with the longer term benefits created for both the consumer and for the community as a whole. For example, if societal marketing had been employed by marketers of baby milk formula, it would not have been sold to African communities where it created financial hardship for those who could ill afford this additional expense. On the other hand, these promotions could have been more beneficially targeted at groups of mothers who were unable to breast-feed for medical or other reasons. By targeting these latter groups, the marketers could have been seen to be acting with social responsibility and offering a social benefit by providing a healthier environment for mothers with infants and perhaps reducing infant mortality.

Societal marketing also includes the idea of marketing being used to address social issues. Governments, regulatory bodies, and charity groups are employing societal marketing to spread information about important social issues, such as in anti-smoking and AIDs awareness campaigns. One of the first examples of the deliberate use of societal marketing to address social ills was a family health programme run by leading businessman, K. T. Chandy in Calcutta, India. He ran an integrated promotional campaign to consumers that advertised the importance of family planning and supported it with the free distribution of high-quality, low-cost condoms, along with training for consumers at the distribution points. This not only helped in reducing family sizes, it also helped with the prevention of the spread of HIV as well as relieving pressure on local health and education services. Societal marketing can also be used to help fundraising for non-governmental organizations (NGOs) and charities working to provide relief for disadvantaged groups. By raising awareness of these important social issues, societal marketing can help to change perceptions and public opinion, by using marketing techniques that are very similar to those used to sell goods and services.

Artificial intelligence

AI is the utilization of a computer to approximate human thinking and learning. Computer programmers write algorithms that provide the computer with the ability to make decisions based on pre-determined options and past actions. For marketing, AI provides a way of leveraging customer data by using machine learning to anticipate customers' needs or their next actions, and to improve the customer journey (see Figure 22).

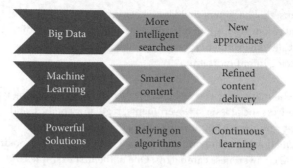

22. Key elements and marketing outcomes of AI.

There has been some exploration around the use of AI in digital marketing. For example, AI can be used to analyse what type of advertising content or copy would be appropriate to 'speak' to a specific target customer group by revealing information about trends and preferences through the analysis of big data. AI can also be used to identify the lifestyle choices of customers regarding their hobbies, favourite celebrities, music choices, and fashions to provide unique content in marketing messages put out through social media. At the same time AI can also be used to generate content for social media posts and chat sites. AI can also provide a bridge between the need of the brand to communicate emotionally with the customer and identifying their rapidly changing needs.

While working at PWC, Norbert Wirth wrote an article on AI where he identified that marketers are equally eager and hesitant in adopting AI, because synthesizing all these different functions presents them with new challenges. AI can help marketers to create clear marketing messages and choose the most attractive marketing mix for each target segment. A specific example would be the use of AI in developing the customer journey by automating all the different touchpoints (when the organization should contact the potential customer) through behavioural analytics so that they are the most effective for that customer or customer group.

The main disadvantage of using AI to respond to customers is that there are concerns about trusting personal interactions to machines, which could lead not only to the subsequent loss of interpersonal connections, but also to a decrease in marketing personnel. Some believe that AI is negatively impacting on the marketer's role by reducing creativity and removing jobs, but they are aware that it is a way of reducing costs and creating new information. By allowing AI to develop content some brand marketers may find that they are losing control over the brand narrative. Algorithms that are used to mimic human interactions are creating many of these concerns, especially as no-one is quite sure what the outcomes of using AI to interact with customers will be.

For AI to be successful, data needs to be accessible, but the use of personal data is becoming more regulated and the automated sharing of data is becoming more difficult. If customers are not willing to share data, AI will be starved of essential information and will not be able to function effectively or employ machine learning to improve its marketing content and communication. Therefore, unless customers are prepared to sign release agreements, the use of AI may become somewhat restricted in the future. Not only can AI help to create the marketing content, but it can also provide a non-intrusive way of delivering the content to the target customers. Data can be gathered on where the customer can be engaged, such as location, devices used, website interactions, and sites visited, to display marketing messages in appropriate forms, including emails, social media posts, pop-up advertisements, and banners at an appropriate frequency. The non-intrusive delivery of the marketing messages in a way that is sensitive to the needs of the target customer is one of the critical challenges to the digital marketer.

Understanding humans may be complicated, but we reveal a considerable amount about what appeals to us through our browsing history. Extending this concept, AI also offers the opportunity to combine personal data (legitimately collected online) with the customer's behaviours, to create personalized advertisements that resonate with consumer emotions and which can interactively engage the customer with AI generated content. AI is an opportunity for marketers to integrate data, skills, and cross-functional organizational expertise to create brands which emotionally connect with their customers and deliver appropriate content in real time to customers wherever they are located.

References

Chapter 1: The nature of marketing

American Marketing Association (2013) https://www.ama.org/the-definition-of-marketing/ (accessed 18 June 2019).

Bordon, B. H. (1964) The concept of the marketing mix, *Journal of Advertising Research* 4(6): 2–7.

Chartered Institute of Marketing (2015) https://www.cim.co.uk/media/4772/7ps.pdf (accessed 18 June 2019)

Doyle, P. (2008) *Value-Based Marketing*, 2nd edn, Chichester: John Wiley & Sons.

Jones, D. and Monierson, D. (1990) Early development of the philosophy of marketing thought, *Journal of Marketing* 54(10): 102–13.

Kotler, P. T., Armstrong, G., Harris, L. C., and Piercy, N. (2017) *Principles of Marketing*, 7th European edn, Harlow: Pearson.

Kohli, A. and Jaworski, B. J. (1990) Market orientation: the construct, research propositions and managerial potential, *Journal of Marketing* 54(2): 1–18.

Levitt, T. (1984) Marketing myopia, *Harvard Business Review* 4(4): 59–80.

McCarthy, E. J. (1964) *Basic Marketing. A Managerial Approach*, Homewood, IL: Irwin.

McLeod, S. (2018) Maslow's hierarchy of needs, https://www.simplypsychology.org/maslow.html (accessed 9 January 2019).

Moorman, C. (2018) Why Apple is still a great marketer and what you can learn, https://www.forbes.com/sites/christinemoorman/2018/01/12/why-apple-is-still-a-great-marketer-and-what-you-can-learn/3ac9ed5e15bd (accessed 3 January 2019).

Maslow, A. H. (1943) A theory of human motivation, *Psychological Review* 50(4): 370–96.

Naver, J. C. and Slater, S. F. (1990) The effect of a market orientation on business profitability, *Journal of Marketing* 54(10): 20–35.

Service marketing: https://www.britannica.com/topic/marketing (accessed 18 June 2019).

Thomas Barratt: https://www.revolvy.com/page/Thomas-J.-Barratt (accessed 3 January 2019).

Kurt Wagner: https://www.vox.com/2017/5/3/15531478/facebook-hiring-3000-people-violent-inappropriate-video-content-post (accessed 29 September 2019).

Chapter 2: Marketing research

American Marketing Association (2014) Marketing research definition, https://www.ama.org/the-definition-of-marketing/ (accessed 11 June 2019).

Babin, B. and Zikmund, W. (2016) *Essentials of Marketing Research*, 6th edn, Boston: Centage Learning.

Bryman, A. (2016) *Social Research Methods*, Oxford: Oxford University Press.

ESOMAR Global Market Research Report (2019) https://www.esomar.org/knowledge-center/library?publication=2898 (accessed 5 August 2019).

Etikan, I. and Bala, K. (2017) Sampling and sampling methods, *Biometrics & Biostatistics International Journal* 5(6): 1–3.

Hair, J. F., Black, W. C., Babin, B., Anderson, R. E., and Tatham, R. L. (2005) *Multivariate Data Analysis*, 6th edn, Upper Sadler River: Prentice-Hall.

Harrell, E. (2019) Neuromarketing: what you need to know, *Harvard Business Review*, https://hbr.org/2019/01/neuromarketing-what-you-need-to-know (accessed 30 August 2019).

Malhotra, N., Nunan, D., and Birks, D. F. (2017) *Marketing Research: An Applied Approach*, 5th edn, Harlow: Pearson.

The New Coke Story: https://www.coca-colacompany.com/stories/coke-lore-new-coke (accessed 6 August 2019).

Parasuraman, A. (1991) *Marketing Research*, 2nd edn, Wokingham: Addison-Wesley.

Chapter 3: Segmentation, targeting, and positioning, and the role of branding

Aaker, D. (1996) *Building Strong Brands*, New York: Free Press.

Barden, P. (2014) *Decoded: The Science Behind Why We Buy*, Chichester: John Wiley & Sons.

Corstjens, M. and Lai, R. (2000) Building store loyalty through store brands, *Journal of Marketing Research* 37(3): 281–91.

Dallenbach, K., Parkinson, J., and Krisjanous, J. (2018) Just how prepared are you? An application of marketing segmentation and theory of planned behavior for disaster preparation, *Journal of Non-profit & Public Sector Marketing* 30(4): 413–43.

Fenton-O'Creevy, M., Dibb, S., and Furnham, A. (2018) Antecedents and consequences of chronic impulsive buying: can impulsive buying be understood as dysfunctional self-regulation? *Psychology & Marketing* 35(3): 175–88.

Freytag, P. V. and Clarke, A. H. (2001) Business to business segmentation, *Industrial Marketing Management* 30(6): 473–86.

Hooley, G., Piercy, N. F., Nicouland, B., and Rudd, J. M. (2017) *Marketing Strategy & Competitive Positioning*, 6th edn, Harlow: Pearson.

Interbrand: https://www.interbrand.com/best-brands/best-global-brands/2019/ranking/#?listFormat=ls (accessed 23 March 2020).

Philip Kotler on branding: https://www.marketingweek.com/philip-kotler-modern-marketing/ (accessed 31 July 2019).

Lanning, M. and Michaels, E. (1988) A business is a value delivery system, *McKinsey Staff Paper*, July: 41.

McDonald M. and Dunbar, L. (2004) *Market Segmentation—How to Do It: How to Profit from It*, Oxford: Elsevier.

Rosenbaum-Elliot, R., Percy, L., and Pervan, S. (2018) *Strategic Brand Management*, 4th edn, Oxford: Oxford University Press.

Stewart, D. W. (1988) Segmentation and positioning for strategic marketing decisions, *Journal of Marketing Research* 35(1): 128–9.

Szmign, I. and Piaentini, M. (2015) *Consumer Behaviour*, Oxford: Oxford University Press.

Wind, Y. and Cardoza, R. (1974) Industrial market segmentation, *Industrial Marketing Management* 3(3): 153–66.

Chapter 4: Consumer and buyer behaviour and the value proposition

Anderson, J. C., Narus, J. A., and Van Rossum, W. (2006) Customer value propositions in business markets, *Harvard Business Review*, May: 90–9.

Ballantyne, D., Frow, P., Varey, R., and Payne, A. (2011) Value propositions as communication practice: taking a wider view, *Industrial Marketing Management* 40(2): 202–10.

Biemans, W. G. (2010) *Business to Business Marketing: A Value-Driven Approach*, Maidenhead: McGraw-Hill.

Capraro, A. J., Broniarczyk, S., and Srivastava, R. K. (2003) Factors influencing the likelihood of customer defection: the role of consumer knowledge, *Journal of the Academy of Marketing Science* 32(2): 164–75.

Cornwell, T. B., Humphreys, M. S., Maguire, A. M., Weeks, C. S., and Tellegen, C. L. (2006) Sponsorship-linked marketing: the role of articulation in memory, *Journal of Consumer Research* 33(3): 312–21.

Engel, J. F., Blackwell, R. D., and Miniard, P. W. (1995) *Consumer Behaviour*, 8th edn, Fort Worth: Dryden.

Keller, K. L. (2013) *Strategic Brand Management*, 4th edn, Harlow: Pearson.

King, S. F. and Burgess, T. F. (2008) Understanding success and failure in customer relationship management, *Industrial Marketing Management* 37(4): 421–31.

Kotler, P. and Armstrong, G. (2017) *Principles of Marketing*, 17th global edn, Harlow: Pearson.

Lanning, M. and Michaels, E. (1988) A business is a value delivery system, *McKinsey Staff Paper*, July: 41.

Payne, A., Frow, P., and Eggart, A. (2017) The customer value proposition: evolution, development and application in marketing, *Journal of the Academy of Marketing Science* 45(4): 467–89.

Pressey, A., Tzokas, N., and Winklhofer, H. (2007) Strategic purchasing and the evaluation of problem key supply relationships: what do key supplies need to know? *Journal of Business & Industrial Marketing* 22(5): 282–94.

Uber value proposition: https://www.wordstream.com/blog/ws/2016/04/27/value-proposition-examples (accessed 6 August 2019).

Webster, F. E. and Wind, Y. (1972) *Organizing Buying Behaviour*, Englewood Cliffs: Prentice Hall.

Wind, Y. and Cardoza, R. (1974) Industrial market segmentation, *Industrial Marketing Management* 3(3): 153–66.

Chapter 5: Promotions (marketing communications) and social media

Advertising Standards Authority codes: https://www.asa.org.uk (accessed 17 January 2019).

De Pelsmaker, P., Geuens, M., and Van Den Bergh, J. (2017) *Marketing Communications: A European Perspective*, 6th edn, Harlow: Pearson.

Duncan, T. (2002) *IMC Using Advertising and Promotion to Build Brands*, Boston: McGraw-Hill Irwin.

Event Marketing Institute (2016) How brands and consumers use events as content generators, http://www.eventmarketer.com/wp-content/uploads/2016/05/2016EventTrackExecSummary.pdf (accessed 11 February 2019).

Fill, C. and Turnbull, S. (2013) *Marketing Communications: Discovery, Creation and Conversations*, 7th edn, Harlow: Pearson.

Global Advertising Spend 2010–18: https://www.statista.com/statistics/236943/global-advertising-spending/ (accessed 16 January 2019).

International Chamber of Commerce, Article C14, Respecting consumer wishes, http://codescentre.iccwbo.org/icc-code/direct-marketing.aspx (accessed 9 February 2019).

Kotler, P. T. and Armstrong, G. (2017) *Principles of Marketing*, 17th edn, Harlow: Pearson.

Kotler, P., Kartajaya, H., and Setiawan, I. (2017) *Marketing 0.4, from Traditional to Digital*, Hoboken, NJ: John Wiley & Sons.

Martin, G. Z. (2017) *The Essential Social Media Marketing Handbook: A New Roadmap for Maximizing Your Brand, Influence, and Credibility*, Wayne, NJ: Careers Press.

Percy, L. and Rosenbaum-Elliott, R. (2016) *Strategic Advertising Management*, 5th edn, Oxford: Oxford University Press.

Public Relations Society of America: https://martech.zone/how-to-measure-public-relations-online/ (accessed 9 February 2019).

Thomas, J. S. and Sullivan, U. Y. (2005) Managing marketing communications with multichannel customers, *Journal of Marketing*, 69(4): 239–5.

Chapter 6: Price and place (managing channels)

Anderson, J. C., Wouters, M., and Van Rossum, W. (2010) Why the highest price isn't the best price, *Sloan Management Review* 51(2): 69–76.

Anderson, P. and Anderson, E. (2002) The new e-commerce intermediaries, *Sloan Management Review* 43(4): 53–62.

De Toni, D., Milan, G. S., Saciloto, E. B., and Larentis, F. (2017) Pricing strategies and levels and their impact on corporate profitability, *Revista de Administracao* 52(2): 120–33.

Gerster, E. (1985) Do higher prices signal higher quality? *Journal of Marketing Research* 22(2): 209–15.

Gourville, J. and Soman, D. (2002) Pricing and the psychology of consumption, *Harvard Business Review* 80(9): 91–6.

Hamilton, R. and Chernev, A. (2013) Low prices are just the beginning: prices image in retail management, *Journal of Marketing* 77(6): 1–20.

Hinterhuber, A. and Liozu, S. (2012) Is it time to rethink your pricing strategy? *Sloan Management Review* 53(4): 69–77.

Kotler, P. and Armstrong, G. (2017) *Principles of Marketing*, 17th global edn, Harlow: Pearson.

Narus, J. A. and Anderson, J. C. (1986) Industrial distributor selling: the roles of outside and inside sales, *Industrial Marketing Management* 15(1): 55–62.

Not for profit vs non-profit—everything you need to know: https://www.upcounsel.com/not-for-profit-vs-nonprofit (accessed 21 August 2019).

Popescu, I. and Wu, Y. (2007) Dynamic pricing strategies with reference effects, *Operations Research* 55(3): ii–613.

Shapiro, B. P. and Jackson, B. B. (1978) Industrial pricing to meet customer needs, *Harvard Business Review*, November/December: 119–27.

Simon, H. (1992) Pricing opportunities-and how to exploit them, *Sloan Management Review* 33(2): 55–65.

Sun, The (newspaper): https://www.thesun.co.uk/travel/5914743/megabus-ads-offering-fares-from-1-have-been-banned-after-the-firm-admitted-as-little-as-one-seat-per-coach-was-available-for-the-price/ (accessed 25 April 2020).

Taylor, D., Brockhaus, S., Knemeyer, A., and Murphy, P. (2019) Omnichannel fulfilment strategies: defining the concept and building an agenda for future inquiry, *The International Journal of Logistics Management* 30(3): 863–89.

Verhoef, P. C., Kannan, P. K., and Inman, J. J. (2015) From multi-channel retailing to omni-channel retailing: introduction to the special issue on multi-channel retailing, *Journal of Retailing* 91(2): 174–81.

Wollenburg, J., Holzapfel, A., Hübner, A., and Kuhn, H. (2018) Configuring retail fulfillment processes for omni-channel customer steering, *International Journal of Electronic Commerce* 22(4): 540–75.

Chapter 7: Product, new product development, and service marketing

Allen, B. J., Dholakia, U. M., and Basuroy, S. (2016) The economic benefits to retailers from customer participation in proprietary web panels, *Journal of Retailing* 92(2): 147–61.

Ansoff, I. (1957) Strategies for diversification, *Harvard Business Review* 35(5): 113–24.

Booms, B. H. and Bitner, M. J. (1981) Marketing strategies and organization structures for service firms. In J. H. Donnelly and W. R. George (eds), *Marketing of Services*, New York: American Marketing Association, pp. 47–51.

Brady, M. K., Baurdeau, B. L., and Heskel, J. (2005) The importance of brand cues in intangible service industries: an application to investment services, *Journal of Service Marketing* 19(6): 401–10.

Buganza, T., Gerst, M., and Verganti, R. (2010) Adoption of NPD flexibility practices in new technology-based firms, *European Journal of Innovation Management* 13(1): 62–80.

Castellion, G. and Markham, S. K. (2013) Myths about new product failure rates, *Journal of Product Innovation & Management* 37(4): 976–9.

Di Benedetto, C. A. (1999) Identifying the key success factors in new product launch, *Journal of Product Innovation Management* 16(3): 530–44.

Furnham, A. and Milner, R. (2013) The impact of mood on customer behaviour: staff mood and environmental factors, *Journal of Retail and Consumer Services* 20(6): 634.

Gill, I., Berenguer, G., and Gevera, A. (2007) The roles of service encounters, service value and job satisfaction in business relationships, *Industrial Marketing Management* 37(8): 921–39.

Gummesson, E. (2004) Implementing the marketing concept: from service and values to lean consumption, *Marketing Theory* 6(3): 291–3.

Jobber, D. and Fahy, J. (2009) *Foundations of Marketing*, Maidenhead: McGraw-Hill.

Philip Kotler's five product levels: https://www.toolshero.com/marketing/five-product-levels-kotler/ (accessed 21 August 2019).

Marinova, D. (2004) Actualising innovation effort: the impact of market knowledge diffusion in a dynamic system of competition, *Journal of Marketing* 68(3): 1–19.

Peres, R., Muller, E., and Mahajan, V. (2010) Innovation diffusion and new product growth models: a critical review and research directions, *International Journal of Research in Marketing* 27(2): 91–106.

Rogers, E. M. (2003) *The Diffusion of Innovations*, 5th edn, New York: The Free Press.

Chapter 8: The changing nature of marketing

Bell, A. (2019) Waiting on hold will soon become a thing of the past, https://whatsnext.nuance.com/customer-experience/artificial-intelligence-bridges-gaps-between-consumer-demands-and-contact-centers/ (accessed 20 August 2019).

Burberry on social media: https://www.business2community.com/social-media/social-media-strategy-rebranding-heritage-at-burberry-02138561 (accessed 27 August 2019).

Chaffey, D. and Smith, P. R. (2017) *Digital Marketing Excellence: Planning Optimizing and Integrating Online Marketing*, London: Routledge.

Charlesworth, A. (2018) *Digital Marketing: A Practical Approach*, Abingdon: Routledge.

Gutierrez, A., O'Leary, S., Rana, N. P., Dwivedi, Y. K., and Calle, T. (2019) Using privacy calculus theory to explore entrepreneurial directions in mobile location-based advertising: identifying intrusiveness as the critical risk factor, *Computers and Human Behavior* 95(6): 295–306.

Heinze, A., Fletcher, G., Rashid, T., and Cruz, A. (2017) *Digital and Social Media Marketing*, London: Routledge.

Kim, A. J. and Ko, E. (2012) Do social media marketing activities enhance customer equity? An empirical study of luxury fashion brand, *Journal of Business Research* 65(10): 1480–6.

Knight, W. (2017) *The Dark Secret at the Heart of AI, Intelligent Machines*, https://www.technologyreview.com/s/604087/ the-dark-secret-at-the-heart-of-ai/ (accessed 29 August 2019).

Kotler, P., Kartajaya, H., and Setiawan, I. (2017) *Marketing 4.0: Moving from Traditional to Digital*, Hoboken, NJ: John Wiley & Sons.

Ramaswamy, V. and Kerimcan, O. (2018) Offerings as digitalized interactive platforms: a conceptual framework and implications, *Journal of Marketing* 82(4): 19–31.

Syam, N. and Sharma, A. (2018) Waiting for a sales renaissance in the fourth industrial revolution: machine learning and artificial intelligence in sales research and practice, *Industrial Marketing Management* 69(2): 135–46.

The most effective social media sites for start-ups: https://www. eu-startups.com/2018/09/the-most-effective-social-media-channelsstrategies-for-startups/ (accessed 27 August 2019).

ten Berg, K., Spil, T. A. M., and Effing, R. (2019) The privacy paradox of utilizing the Internet of Things and Wi-Fi tracking in smart cities. In Y. Dwivedi, E. Ayaburi, R. Boateng, and J. Effah (eds), *ICT Unbounded, Social Impact of Bright ICT Adoption: TDIT 2019. IFIP Advances in Information and Communication Technology*, vol. 558, Cham: Springer.

Wirth, N. (2018) Hello marketing, what can artificial intelligence help you with? *International Journal of Market Research* 60(5): 435–8.

Further reading

Chapter 1: The nature of marketing

Christopher, M., Payne, A., and Ballantyne, D. (2002) *Relationship Marketing: Creating Stakeholder Value*, 2nd edn, Oxford: Butterworth Heinemann.

Gronroos, C. and Volma, P. (2013) Critical service logic: making sense of value creation and co-creation, *Journal of the Academy of Marketing Science* 41(2): 133–50.

Kumar, V., Jones, E., Venkatatesan, R., and Leone, R. P. (2011) Is market orientation a source of sustainable competitive advantage or simply the cost of competing? *Journal of Marketing* 75(2): 16–40.

Maslow, A. H. (1943) A theory of human motivation, *Psychological Review* 50(4): 370–96.

Piercy N. (2017) *Market-Led Strategic Change: Transforming the Process of Going to Market*, 5th edn, Abingdon: Routledge.

Vargo, S. L. and Lush, R. F. (2008) A service-dominant logic: continuing the evolution, *Journal of the Academy of Marketing Science* 36(1): 1–10.

Chapter 2: Marketing research

Bryman, A. (2016) *Social Research Methods*, Oxford: Oxford University Press.

Churchill, G. A., Jr, and Iacobucci, D. (2002) *Marketing Research Methodological Foundations*, 8th edn, Mason: South-Western.

Hair, J. F., Black, W. C., Babin, B., Anderson, R. E., and Tatham, R. L. (2005) *Multivariate Data Analysis*, 6th edn, Upper Sadler River: Prentice-Hall.

Harrell, E. (2019) Neuromarketing: what you need to know, *Harvard Business Review* https://hbr.org/2019/01/neuromarketing-what-you-need-to-know

Malhotra, N., Nunan, D., and Birks, D. F. (2017) *Marketing Research: An Applied Approach*, 5th edn, Harlow: Pearson.

Chapter 3: Segmentation, targeting, and positioning, and the role of branding

Baumgartner, H. (2002) Towards a personology of the consumer, *Journal of Consumer Research* 29(2): 286–93.

Fuchs, C. and Diamantopoulos, A. (2010) Evaluating the effectiveness of brand-positioning strategies from a consumer perspective, *European Journal of Marketing* 44(11–12): 1763–86.

Gensler, S., Volckner, F., Liu-Thompkins, Y., and Wiertz, C. (2013) Managing brands in a social media environment, *Journal of Interactive Marketing* 27(4): 242–56.

Keller, K. L. (2013) *Strategic Brand Management*, 4th edn, Harlow: Pearson.

Rosenbaum-Elliot, R., Percy, L., and Pervan, S. (2018) *Strategic Brand Management*, 4th edn, Oxford: Oxford University Press.

Chapter 4: Consumer and buyer behaviour and the value proposition

Biemans, W. G. (2010) *Business to Business Marketing: A Value-Driven Approach*, Maidenhead: McGraw-Hill.

Payne, A., Frow, P., and Eggart, A. (2017) The customer value proposition: evolution, development and application in marketing, *Journal of the Academy of Marketing Science* 45(4): 467–89.

Soloman, M. R. (2016) *Consumer Behaviour: Buying, Having and Being*, Harlow: Pearson.

Chapter 5: Promotions (marketing communications) and social media

De Pelsmaker, P., Geuens, M., and Van Den Bergh, J. (2017) *Marketing Communications: A European Perspective*, 6th edn, Harlow: Pearson.

Duncan, T. R. and Everett, S. E. (1993) Client perceptions of integrated marketing communications, *Journal of Advertising Research* 33(6/7): 30–9.

Percy, L. and Rosenbaum-Elliott, R. (2016) *Strategic Advertising Management*, 5th edn, Oxford: Oxford University Press.

Chapter 6: Price and place (managing channels)

Grewal, D., Ailawadi, K. L., Gauri, D., Hall, K., Kopalle, P., and Robertson, J. R. (2011) Innovations in retail pricing and promotions, *Journal of Retailing* 87(S1): S43–52.

Popescu, I. and Wu, Y. (2007) Dynamic pricing strategies with reference effects, *Operations Research* 55(3): ii–613.

Shapiro, B. P. and Jackson, B. B. (1978) Industrial pricing to meet customer needs, *Harvard Business Review* 56 (November/December): 119–27.

Souder, W. E. (1987) *Managing New Product Innovations*, New York: Lexington Books.

Chapter 7: Product, new product development, and service marketing

Lund, D. L. and Marinova, D. (2014) Management revenue across retail channels: the interplay of service performance and direct marketing, *Journal of Marketing* 78(5): 99–118.

Mayer, C. and Schwager, A. (2007) Understanding customer experience, *Harvard Business Review* 85(2): 177–94.

Thomas, J. S. and Sullivan, U. Y. (2005) Managing marketing communications with a multichannel customer, *Journal of Marketing* 69(4): 239–51.

Wirtz, J. and Lovelock, C. (2016) *Services Marketing*, 8th edn, Hackensack: World Scientific.

Chapter 8: The changing nature of marketing

Dwivedi, Y. K., Hughes, L., Ismagilova, E., Le Meunier-FitzHugh, K., et al. (in press) Artificial intelligence (AI): multidisciplinary perspectives on emerging challenges, opportunities, and agenda for research and practice, *International Journal of Information Management*.

Heinze, A., Fletcher, G., Rashid, T., and Cruz, A. (2017) *Digital and Social Media Marketing*, London: Routledge.

Homburg, C., Jozic, D., and Kuehnl, C. (2017) Customer experience management: toward implementing an evolving marketing concept, *Journal of the Academy of Marketing Science* 45(3): 377–401.

Kotler, P., Kartajaya, H., and Setiawan, I. (2017) *Marketing 4.0: Moving from Traditional to Digital*, Hoboken, NJ: John Wiley & Sons.

Lehman, D. R. and Jocz, K. E. (1997) *Reflections on the Future of Marketing, Practice and Education*, Cambridge: Marketing Science Institute.

Martin, G. Z. (2017) The *Essential Social Media Marketing Handbook: A New Roadmap for Maximizing your Brand, Influence, and Credibility*, Wayne, NJ: Career Press.

Singh, J., Flaherty, K., Sohi, R. S., Deeter-Schmelz, D., Habel, J., Le Meunier-FitzHugh, K., Malshe, A., Mullins, R., and Onyemah. V. (2019) Sales profession and professionals in the age of digitization and artificial technologies: concepts, priorities, and questions, *Journal of Personal Selling and Sales Management* 39(1): 2–22.

Index

For the benefit of digital users, indexed terms that span two pages
(e.g., 52–53) may, on occasion, appear on only one of those pages.

A

additions 105
advertising 67–70
  billboards 4–5
  continuous marketing 54
  ethics 123–5
  television 4–6
advertising research 18
Advertising Standards Authority
  (ASA) 86
airline industry 62
algorithms 129
Alibaba 77, 91–2, 119
Amazon 45, 77, 90–2, 119
American Marketing
  Association 1–2, 16–17
Ansoff, Igor 107–8
Apple Corporation 8–9, 14, 27,
  31–2, 35–6, 45
artificial intelligence (AI) 127–30
Aston Martin 69
AT&T 73–4
Audi 33

augmented marketing mix (seven
  Ps) 13–15, 97–8
augmented products 98–9

B

Barratt, Thomas James 4
behavioural segmentation 34, 36–7
behaviour of B2B buyers 55–8
behaviour of consumers 50–5
Bentley cars 41
Bernays, Edward 72
Biemans, Wim 57–8
big data 27–8, 117–18, 128–9
billboard advertising 4–5
Bitner, Mary 109
BMW 33
Booms, Bernard 109
Boston Consulting Company
  (BCC) 100–2
BP 86
brand association 18
branding 31–2, 43–6

brand stories 23–4
brand tribes 35–7
Breitling 86
British Airways 14–15, 37, 42–3, 62, 111–12
bundling (pricing strategy) 87–8
Burberry 117
business-to-business (B2B) marketing 6–7, 37–41
buyer behaviour 55–8
sales promotions 71; *see also* sales promotions
business-to-consumer (B2C) marketing 6–7
buy class 57–8
buyer decision-making 18, 55–8
buyer–seller relationship 121–2

C

Cadbury Chocolate 68
capabilities of organizations 15
car industry
segmentation identification 33
targeted marketing 41
Castellion, George 106–7
Cathay Pacific 62
celebrity endorsements 70
Chandy, K. T. 127
Chanel 86
channels
consumer, industrial and service 95–6
direct and indirect 80–1
distribution 80–1, 89–92
multi-channel 94–5
omni-channel 95
charities 7, 82, 127
clothing industry 37
cluster sampling 26
Coca-Cola 7, 29, 31–2, 40–1, 44–5, 93
co-creation of value 8

Colgate 45–6
communication process 66–7; *see also* promotions
company size segmentation 39
comparison sites 52, 54, 92, 111–12
competition-based pricing 83, 86
complementary pricing 84
concept testing 18
consumer apathy 68–9
consumer channels 95–6
consumers 6
behaviour 50–5
vs. customers 3
decision-making process 47–55
motivation 48
sales promotions 71; *see also* sales promotions
continuous marketing 54
convenience sampling 25
cookies 78
core products 98–9
cost-based pricing 83
cost-plus approach 81–2
culture, and decision-making 50–1
customer forums 78
customer insights 27–8
customers
vs. consumers 3
innovators 107
needs, wants, and demands 9–10
price demands 81–2
segmentation identification 30–40
customer satisfaction research 18
customer value 7–9, 58
customized targeting 41

D

Daellenback, Kate 35–6
data analysis 28–9
data collection 21–2, 25–8
data sources 19–21

decision-making process 47–55
  B2B buyers 55–8
Deliveroo 116
delivery companies 91–2
demand forecasting 18
demographic segmentation 33–5
desk research 20
differential pricing 84, 86
differentiated targeting 41
differentiation 27, 98
digital marketing 76–9;
    see also social media
  artificial intelligence (AI)
    in 127–30
digitization 117–21
direct marketing 74–5
disaster planning 35–6
Disney 45
distribution 80–1, 89–92
  international 123
  methods 92–4
  multi-channel 94–5
  omni-channel 95
  trends 18
diversification 108
Doyle, Peter 7–8
dynamic pricing 84, 86–7, 119–20
Dyson 45–6, 88–9, 101–2, 105, 108

E

easyJet 62
eBay 91–2
Effing, Robin 125–6
ESOMAR 17
ethics 123–7
Event Marketing Institute 75
events marketing 75–6
exchange process 2
exclusive distribution 93–4
exhibitions 75–6
expected products 100
experiments 23–4

F

Facebook 77–9, 114–15
fast-moving consumer goods
    (FMCGs) 2–3
field data research 20–2
  sampling 24–5
financial goals 82
focused targeting 41
focus groups 22
follow-my-leader pricing 84
Ford 41
formal products 98–9
for-profit organizations 82
four Ps (Promotion, Price, Place,
    and Product) 4–7, 10–15,
    32, 53, 118
free samples 71–2
Frow, Penny 60–1
fuel market 86, 96
functional value 7–8
Furnham, Adrian 112
future of marketing 114–30

G

Gaultier, Jean-Paul 40
General Motors 73–4
geographic segmentation 34–5, 38
Global Advertising Spend 68–9
globalization 7, 122–3
goods, vs. services 2–3, 97–8, 110
Google 45, 77
Google AdWords 116
Google Analytics 76–7
growth matrix 107–8
Gummersson, Evert 109

H

Harley-Davidson 50–1
headline title 60
Heinz 11–12

Hello magazine 89
hierarchy of needs 9–10
Hoover UK 71
Huawei 27, 35–6

I

India, societal marketing 127
industrial channels 95–6
industry type segmentation 38–9
influences on consumers'
    behaviour 51–5
information evaluation 48–9, 54
information search 48–9, 54
information sources 19–21
innovators 107
Intel 43
intermediaries 90–2
international marketing 6–7,
    122–4
Internet intelligence 18
Internet of Things 117–18,
    125–6
Internet sites
    distribution 91–2
    ethics 125
interviews 22–3
Irn-Bru 44

J

Jackson, Barbara B. 83
Jaguar/Land Rover 33
James Bond films 69
Jobber, David 104–5
John Lewis and Partners 69–70
judgemental sampling 26
Just Eat 116

K

KFC 72–3
Kotler, Philip 1–2, 31, 46,
    50, 60, 100
Krisjanous, Jayne 35–6

L

Lacoste 35–6
language problems 123
Lanning, Michael 43, 58
launch events 72
Lidl 86
lifecycle of products 97, 102–4
loss leaders 71–2
low-cost pricing 86
loyalty 37
loyalty cards 54–5, 117–18
Lufthansa 62

M

McCarthy, E. Jerome 4–6
McDonalds 35–6, 45
machine learning 127–8
macro segmentations 38
Mailchimp 59
management information systems
    (MISs) 19–20
market-based pricing 83–4
marketing 12–13
    definition 1–4
    origins and history 4–6
    services 13–15
marketing analytics 18
marketing communications *see*
    promotions
marketing mix (four Ps) 4–7,
    10–15, 32, 53, 118 *see*
    Augmented Marketing Mix
    (seven Ps)
marketing promotions *see*
    promotions
marketing research 16–29
    misinterpretations 29
    process 25–7
    types 18
marketing strategy 4–7, 26–7
market-orientated approach 8–9
market positioning 18
market research 16

Marketing

Markham, Stephen 106–7
Marks & Spencer 31, 69–70
Marmite 107–8
    new product development
        (NPD) 105
    taste tests 22
mass distribution 92–3
media events 72–3, 75–6
Megabus 86–7
Mercedes-Benz 33, 45
message 66–70
Michaels, Edward 43, 58
micro segmentations 38–40
Microsoft 12, 45
Milner, Rebecca 112
mobile phone companies 27–8,
    35–6, 123
monetary value 7–8
motivations of consumers 48
multi-channel distribution 94–5
multinational enterprises
    (MNEs) 39
mystery shopping 18, 23

N

needs, wants, and demands 9–10
neuromarketing 24
new product development
    (NPD) 97, 104–7
new product lines 105
new to the world products 105
Nike 35–6
Nokia 123
non-governmental organizations
    (NGOs) 127
non-probability sampling 25–6
North Face clothing 42–3
not-for-profit marketing 6–7
not-for-profit organizations 82

O

observations 23
offers *see* sales promotions

OK magazine 89
Olympic sponsorship 74
omni-channel distribution 95
online panels 18
online reviews 52, 54, 92, 111–12
opinion leaders 52, 70

P

Panasonic 74
Parkinson, Joy 35–6
Payne, Adrian 60–1
Pears' soap 4–5
penetration pricing 84, 89
personal selling 76
place 12, 80–1, 89–94
Porsche 33, 93–4
Porter, Michael 27
positioning 41–3
post-purchase evaluation
    47–50, 54–5
potential products 100
predatory pricing 84
premium-based pricing 84, 86
price 13, 80
    digitization 119–20
    of services 112–13
price elasticity 18
price leadership 84
price skimming 84, 88–9
pricing strategies 81–8
    mistakes 88
    temporary 84, 88–9
Primark 86
primary research 20–2
    sampling 24–5
privacy paradox 125–6
probability sampling 24–6
problem-identification
    research 17–19
problem recognition 48
problem-solving research
    17–19
process, digitization 120–1
Procter & Gamble 100

product placement 69, 91
product portfolio 100–2
product replacements 105
products 3, 11–12, 97
  constituents 98–100
  definition 98–100
  lifecycle 97, 102–4
  new product development
    (NPD) 97, 104–7
  positioning 41–3
product strategy 107–9
promotional mix 65
promotional pricing 84, 89
promotions 12–13, 63–79
  advertising *see* advertising
  communication process 66–7
  digital marketing 76–9;
    see also social media
  digitization 120
  direct marketing 74–5
  events marketing 75–6
  personal selling 76
  public relations (PR) 63, 72–3
  sales promotions 70–2
  sponsorship 73–4
psychographic segmentation 34–6
psychological value 7–8
public relations (PR) 63, 72–3
Public Relations Society of
    America 73
public services 7
pull strategy 90–1
purposive sampling 26
push strategy 90–1

Q

qualitative data 21–3
quality, reflected in price 80
quantitative data 20–1, 28–9
questionnaires 21–2
quota sampling 25–6

R

rating sites 52, 54, 92, 111–12
reference groups 51–2
research 16–29
  misinterpretations 29
  process 25–7
  types 18
Ryanair 62

S

Sainsbury's 86
sales forecasting 18
salespeople 76, 121–2
sales promotions 70–2, 88
sampling 24–6
Samsung 27, 35–6, 45
secondary research 20
segmentation
    identification 18, 30–40
selection bias 24–5
selective attention 68–9
selective distribution 93
service channels 95–6
service marketing 6–7
services 12
  digitization 118
  vs. goods 2–3, 97–8, 110
  marketing 13–15, 109–13
  online 119
  products 99
seven Ps (four Ps plus
    People, Physical
    Evidence, and
    Processes) 13–15, 97–8
Shapiro, Benson P. 83
share of voice 67
Shell Corporation 86
Siemens 41
skimming 84, 88–9
snowball sampling 26

social media 12–13, 64, 76–9,
    114–17
  ethics 125
social value 7–8
societal marketing 115, 126–7
SofaSofa 118
Sony 27
Southwest Airlines 62
Spil, Ton 125–6
sponsorship 73–4
start-up companies 116
Steinway Grand Pianos 104
store audits 18
stratified sampling 24–6
subcultures 50–1
surveys 21–2

T

targeted marketing 30, 40–1, 67
tech-based businesses 115–16
temporary pricing
    strategies 84, 88–9
ten Berg, Krystan 125–6
Tencent 77
Tesco 30, 56–7, 86, 117–18
test marketing 18
Toyota 7, 45

trade fairs 75
train travel, differential pricing 86
travel industry 35–6, 86, 118
trend spotting 18
TripAdvisor 54, 111–12
Trustpilot 92
TV advertising 4–6

U

Uber 60–1, 116
undifferentiated targeting 40–1
Unilever 7, 22, 122–3

V

value 7–9
value proposition 43, 58–62

W

Walmart 56–7
Wirth, Norbert 128
Woods, Tiger 73–4

Y

YouTube 77

ADVERTISING
A Very Short Introduction
Winston Fletcher

The book contains a short history of advertising and an explanation of how the industry works, and how each of the parties (the advertisers , the media and the agencies) are involved. It considers the extensive spectrum of advertisers and their individual needs. It also looks at the financial side of advertising and asks how advertisers know if they have been successful, or whether the money they have spent has in fact been wasted. Fletcher concludes with a discussion about the controversial and unacceptable areas of advertising such as advertising products to children and advertising products such as cigarettes and alcohol. He also discusses the benefits of advertising and what the future may hold for the industry.

INFORMATION
A Very Short Introduction
Luciano Floridi

Luciano Floridi, a philosopher of information, cuts across many subjects, from a brief look at the mathematical roots of information - its definition and measurement in 'bits'- to its role in genetics (we are information), and its social meaning and value. He ends by considering the ethics of information, including issues of ownership, privacy, and accessibility; copyright and open source. For those unfamiliar with its precise meaning and wide applicability as a philosophical concept, 'information' may seem a bland or mundane topic. Those who have studied some science or philosophy or sociology will already be aware of its centrality and richness. But for all readers, whether from the humanities or sciences, Floridi gives a fascinating and inspirational introduction to this most fundamental of ideas.

'Splendidly pellucid.'

Steven Poole, The Guardian

PRIVACY
A Very Short Introduction
Raymond Wacks

Professor Raymond Wacks is a leading international expert
on privacy. For more than three decades he has published
numerous books and articles on this controversial subject.
Privacy is a fundamental value that is under attack from several
quarters. Electronic surveillance, biometrics, CCTV, ID cards,
RFID codes, online security, the monitoring of employees,
the uses and misuses of DNA, - to name but a few - all raise
fundamental questions about our right to privacy. This *Very Short
Introduction* also analyzes the tension between free speech
and privacy generated by intrusive journalism, photography,
and gratuitous disclosures by the media of the private lives
of celebrities. Professor Wacks concludes this stimulating
introduction by considering the future of privacy in our society.

www.oup.com/vsi

WRITING AND SCRIPT
A Very Short Introduction
Andrew Robinson

Without writing, there would be no records, no history, no books, and no emails. Writing is an integral and essential part of our lives; but when did it start? Why do we all write differently and how did writing develop into what we use today? All of these questions are answered in this *Very Short Introduction*. Starting with the origins of writing five thousand years ago, with cuneiform and Egyptian hieroglyphs, Andrew Robinson explains how these early forms of writing developed into hundreds of scripts including the Roman alphabet and the Chinese characters.

'User-friendly survey.'

Steven Poole, The Guardian

STATISTICS
A Very Short Introduction
David J. Hand

Modern statistics is very different from the dry and dusty discipline of the popular imagination. In its place is an exciting subject which uses deep theory and powerful software tools to shed light and enable understanding. And it sheds this light on all aspects of our lives, enabling astronomers to explore the origins of the universe, archaeologists to investigate ancient civilisations, governments to understand how to benefit and improve society, and businesses to learn how best to provide goods and services. Aimed at readers with no prior mathematical knowledge, this *Very Short Introduction* explores and explains how statistics work, and how we can decipher them.

www.oup.com/vsi